A LEADER LED

A LEADER LED

A Devotional Study of I Timothy

by
GUY H. KING

CHRISTIAN LITERATURE CRUSADE
FORT WASHINGTON   PENNSYLVANIA 19034

CHRISTIAN LITERATURE CRUSADE

U.S.A.
Box 1449, Fort Washington, PA 19034

CANADA
Box 189, Elgin, Ontario KOG 1EO

Copyright©Marshall, Morgan & Scott, Ltd.
Renewed 1962

First published 1951
First American edition 1970

This Printing 1988

ISBN 0-87508-283-1

This edition published under special
arrangement with
Marshall, Morgan & Scott, Ltd.
3 Beggarwood Lane
Basingstoke, Hants., RG23 TCP

PRINTED IN THE UNITED STATES OF AMERICA

FOREWORD

THIS book is issued in response to many requests from those who, having had the work on II Timothy—*To My Son*—have desired another volume on I Timothy. So here it is, launched in the feeling of one of Shakespeare's characters—" 'Tis a poor thing, but mine own ! "

One of the impressions these studies have made on me is that, while the Epistle is written to a particular person, and to meet peculiar circumstances, it yet has such wide application to ourselves, and to our own conditions of life, which I have tried to bring out all the way through.

If God can use the book I shall greatly rejoice.

G. H. K.

CHRIST CHURCH VICARAGE,
BECKENHAM

CONTENTS

I

DEAR CHILD AND DOUGHTY COMRADE

I TIMOTHY i. 1-4

1 Paul, an apostle of Jesus Christ by the commandment of God our Saviour, and Lord Jesus Christ, *which is* our hope ;

2 Unto Timothy, *my* own son in the faith :   Grace, mercy, *and* peace, from God our Father and Jesus Christ our Lord.

3 As I besought thee to abide still at Ephesus, when I went into Macedonia, that thou mightest charge some that they teach no other doctrine.

4 Neither give heed to fables and endless genealogies, which minister questions, rather than godly edifying which is in faith : *so do.*

THE intimate friendship between Paul and Timothy is one of the most beautiful comradeships in all history.   The one is thirty years older than the other ; but there is a respectively paternal and filial relationship the one to the other that is delightful to behold.   " Dear child, and doughty comrade " : yes, that about sums up the feeling of the elder member of this partnership for his young helper.   Timothy is now assuming a position of great responsibility ;   he is given the Oversight of the Church at Ephesus—a task especially onerous for a young man of only thirty-five years, and a man delicate, timid, and sensitive, at that.   Paul is only too well aware of the problems and perils of the situation ;   and he writes this Letter to give to his protégé guidance, and good cheer.   As we take up the Epistle, and begin our study of its contents, we notice, at once, the way—

PAUL INTRODUCES HIMSELF

First, of course, (i) *By his Name.*   Like all Eastern correspondents, he opens with it.   We stay to remark that (*a*) He was known first as Saul—his Hebrew name.   " An Hebrew of the Hebrews ", he describes himself, in Philippians iii. 5, and if, as we shall see, he afterwards dropped the use of his patronymic, we can be quite sure that it was not out of any lessening of pride and affection for his national birthright.   Indeed, all through his life and ministry he maintained his love for his own people, and his longing for their welfare. Wherever he went, his first " port of call " was always the synagogue. However wide-flung was his message, it was always " to the Jew first ", Romans i. 16. Whatever other enthusiasms he had, this was amongst his foremost, " My heart's desire and prayer to GOD for Israel is, that they might be saved ", Romans x. 1. Incidentally, what interesting Bible studies can be got by the comparison of the contrasted careers of people bearing the same name. Take the Ananiases, for instance : Ananias, the deceitful, Acts v. 1 ; Ananias, the disgraceful, Acts xxiii. 2 ; and Ananias, the delightful, Acts ix. 10. And here, what a contrast is seen between the Old Testament Saul and the New Testament Saul—the end of the one, " I have played the fool ", I Samuel xxvi. 21 ; and of the other, " I have fought a good fight ", II Timothy iv. 7. (b) But now, long since, " Saul, the Church's spoiler ", as John Ellerton's hymn describes him, has become Paul, the Church's founder, in so many places. This latter is, of course, his Roman cognomen, given him by virtue of his being a Roman citizen, Acts xxii. 25–8. " Saul, who also is called Paul ", xiii. 9–I cannot help thinking that the " also " implies " like Sergius Paulus ", of verse 7 ; but, of course, he " also " had that second name as well as his first. You see, he has just started out on his specific and specialised ministry as the apostle of the Gentiles, and what more natural than that he should thenceforward use his Gentile name ? From then on, therefore, he has been known as Paul—and it is that name which has become so dear to young Timothy, and with which his beloved mentor begins the so precious Letter.

Not only thus, but also (ii) *By his Office*—he here introduces himself. Paul sets great store by his position, and holds it in high regard. " I magnify mine office ", he says, in Romans xi. 13. So he reminds Timothy that he is (a) ": An apostle of JESUS CHRIST ". There are different sorts of apostleship. Paul was not of the original band, the Twelve ; but he was none the less an apostle, as he claims in so many of his Epistles. I observe that, in Galatians i. 19, James, the LORD's brother is stated to be an apostle ; as, too, is Barnabas, in Acts xiv. 14. Indeed, it is not too greatly stretching the figure if we say that all we Christians may be called apostles, inasmuch as the word itself means " a sent-one ". Each of us believers is intended to be at GOD's disposal, that He may despatch us hither and thither upon His errands. That is a delightful description that Gabriel gives of himself, in Luke i. 19—" I am Gabriel, that stand in the presence of GOD ; and am sent to speak unto thee, and to shew thee these glad tidings ". Stand—ready for orders ; Sent—on His errand ; Speak—a message from Him ; Show—in the angel's case, to show by the expression of the word ; in our case, to show by the embodiment of the word in our life and conduct. Yes, all of us as apostles, in this sense : such is the Master's purpose and ideal for us. But, of course, Paul's apostolate was of a particular order and kind, quite different from what we have just been considering as properly belonging to ourselves. Notice that his office was conferred (b) " By the appointment of GOD ". Timothy is not for one moment to suppose that Paul has taken this responsibility upon himself, that he is self-appointed to his task ; rather has it been thrust upon him by the Master, who, right at the commencement, had said, " he is a chosen vessel unto Me ", Acts ix. 15. He is what he is " By Royal Appointment ". So it is to be noted that what he shall subsequently say will, though all spoken in love, be uttered with authority, having behind it all the weight of the Divine imprimatur.

One further point. He introduces himself (iii) *By his Possessions* —" our ", is his word. Who is it that said that " Christianity is a religion of personal pronouns " ? Paul is prolific in his use of them ; so, too, is the Psalmist. Normally, the apostle would have said " My " ; but just now he links himself up with Timothy, and because they both alike share in these blessed possessions, he says " Our ". How grand it is when we get alongside a fellow-believer, and, talking together of the things of GOD, can say " Our ". So here it is, (a) " Our Saviour "—this is the first and fundamental connection between GOD and the believer. It is as our Saviour that we must first come to know Him, bringing us pardon for sin's guilt, cleansing from sin's stain, victory over sin's power, release from sin's hold. Then comes (b) " Our Lord " —for His lordship should inevitably ensue from His saviourhood. He has a blood-bought right over the soul that He has redeemed. I see that the Revised Version has omitted the word " Lord " ; but the fact is there, even if the word be absent— and certainly it seems that manuscript authority justifies the Revisers' decision. Yet, we have no hesitation in keeping to the Authorised Version, particularly as, in the very next verse, the phrase " our Lord " is found, both in A.V. and R.V. But, to return to the personal, and practical point of view, is He, as a matter of fact, our Lord ? We remember that His lordship makes an all-out, and all-in, demand upon our whole life and

being. The words written on the fly-leaf of a university under-
graduate are still true—

" If you do not crown Him lord of all,
  You do not really crown Him lord at all."

Paul, then, reminds Timothy they share a common possession of
a wonderful Saviour, and a mighty Lord ; and, another thing,
He is (c) " Our Hope "—No other religion than Christianity
possesses this characteristic of hope. The pessimism of Buddhism,
or the fatalism of Mohammedanism, are, by their very nature,
debarred from, devoid of, anything like this trait of blessed
expectation. As the late Dr. G. H. Morrison said, " In its
radiant quality of hope, the gospel of JESUS stands alone ".
Well, He not only gives, but " is ", our hope. What hope is
there for this poor distraught, distracted world ? He is our hope.
What hope is there for the sinful, unsaved man ? He is our hope.
What hope is there of our being able to serve GOD aright ? He
is our hope. What hope is there for us of any happy hereafter ?
He is our hope. In all sorts of ways, as Romans viii. 24 says,
" We are saved by hope "—The International Hope, the Redeem-
ing Hope, the Pentecostal Hope, the Advent Hope. Our love
goes out to Him, who is our Saviour ; our loyalty is fixed on Him,
who is our Lord ; our light proceeds from Him, who is our Hope.
Yes, Timothy, would Paul say, Yours and Mine—" our " !
And now—

PAUL INDUCTS HIS YOUNG COLLEAGUE

In these next succeeding verses, 2–4, you have the first steps
which culminated eventually in the moment when " Youth
takes the Helm " Dwell, first, on (i) *His relationship* to Paul.
" My own son in the faith ". See (a) How it happened. In the
course of his First Missionary Journey, Paul came to the city
of Lystra, where lived a godly family—a Greek gentleman and
his Jewish wife and their little son, " Tiny Tim ", Acts xvi. 1 ;
granny also seems to have lived with them, II Timothy i. 5.
By the time the great evangelist came to their home town,
Tim has grown to be a boy of fifteen. He had enjoyed a carefully
religious upbringing, based upon the Old Testament Scriptures,
II Timothy iii. 15 ; and now this preacher had come to the place,
and was showing how those Old Prophecies all pointed on to the
Coming of the Lord JESUS, the promised Messiah—in other

words, as Acts xiv. 7 has it, he " preached the gospel ". We do not know much about the results of the mission, how many conversions there were ; but it seems that one of the " fruits " was this boy Timothy, whom Paul had the joy of winning to CHRIST. Joy ? Yes, indeed, for there is no happiness on earth comparable to the delight of getting a soul for the Saviour. It is a task worth the putting our all into, for, as Proverbs xi. 30 teaches us, " He that winneth souls is wise ". Perhaps we may add that especially is that true when it is a young soul that is won. When, upon one occasion, on returning from a meeting, D. L. Moody told his hosts that there were two and a half conversions they smilingly said, " Oh yes, two adults and a child, presumably ? " But Mr. Moody answered, " Oh no, two children and an adult." He felt—and was he not right ?—that the conversion of a grown-up is the capturing for CHRIST of but half a life, the first half being already spent, and wasted ; while the turning of a little one to Him was the securing of a whole life. Oh, you who read these lines, and covet to be soul winners, get after the children—it is highest wisdom. Paul never did finer work for the Kingdom than when he " landed " young Timothy " in the net ". See (b) How he developed. Is child conversion a merely ephemeral emotionalism, that soon wears off ? I who write this book was converted as a boy of fourteen. I beat Timothy by a year ! Alas, I haven't been anything like what I ought to have been, but I can at least testify that it doesn't wear off. And, in a much, much higher class, Timothy is another example of the truth that it lasts—just because He lasts. Look a moment at Acts xvi. 2, which says that he " was well reported of by the brethren ". Six years have passed since Paul had his mission there ; and as he here returns, it is so natural that he should enquire how the converts have stood. " What about young Timothy ? " he asks, " how has he gone on ? " How his heart would kindle at the report they gave—a good report ; for he would share John's feeling, in III John 4, " I have no greater joy than to hear that my children walk in truth ". Timothy has grown " well " as a Christian ; and now he is twenty-one years old, ready for further and wider service. So note (c) How he joined up. " Him would Paul have to go forth with him ", Acts xvi. 3. The young man was under no illusion as to what was involved in this discipleship ; he not only guessed but actually knew something of what the cost was likely to be. For he had heard of, and possibly seen, the stoning of Paul on that first visit, that time when, as a boy, he had been led to CHRIST.

Persecution, hardship, suffering, death perhaps—but this young man, delicate, sensitive, timid though he be, as we have seen, is ready to face it all. Anything; anywhere; any cost—such is the intrepid spirit of this young crusader. How many of us have such courageous consecration to the out and out service of the Master ? So Timothy joins Paul's party, which is thereby made complete once more. Silas, for Barnabas, Acts xv. 40 ; and now Timothy for John Mark. It is interesting to observe that Paul seemed always to love to have a youngster on his party—presumably, that he might train them to take over when he and his older helpers fell out, through death, or age, or infirmity. This old campaigner was ever a great strategist ! So this dear child becomes the doughty comrade. From now on, he is most closely associated with his revered leader—who ordained him for his ministry " by the putting on of my hands ", II Timothy i. 6 ; who, in course of time, testified that " as a son with the father, he hath served with me in the gospel ", Philippians ii. 22 ; and who, at the end, longed to have him at his side, " Do thy diligence to come shortly unto me. . . . Do thy diligence to come before winter ", II Timothy iv. 9 and 21.

Next we take note of (ii) *His work for God.* In the course of the missionary annals we find him accompanying Paul at Corinth, at Ephesus, at Athens, at Antioch, at Philippi, at Rome—the maritime city, the oriental city, the philosophical city, the commercial city, the colonial city, the imperial city, as T. A. Gurney describes them. In such varied environments would Timothy gain great experience that will serve him in good stead when, later on, bereft of his leader's presence, he has to tackle, on his own, the perplexities and perils of his Ephesian episcopate. Truly, there is no experience that comes to us in life that cannot be laid under tribute to equip us the better for the service of GOD. As a side-light upon the way in which he had travelled round with the apostle, we find that Timothy's name is associated with Paul's in no less than six of his Epistles. We find, moreover, that Timothy had so grown in tact, and in spiritual acumen, that Paul uses him to go and tackle delicate situations. Such is the sort of situation that he is called upon to meet in our verse 3, " I besought thee to abide still at Ephesus, when I went into Macedonia, that thou mightest charge some that they teach no other doctrine." It is a sort of induction into the office that he is afterwards to occupy, a kind of foretaste of the problems of his future Oversight.

In view of what is, and what will be, involved, we are not

surprised that Timothy is here encouraged by (iii) *His blessings for life*. Paul's wish for him is also a prayer—a threefold intercession that, in the midst of the outward troubles and turmoils that will assuredly meet him, he may have the inward blessings that shall at all times, and in all circumstances, keep his heart at rest. (*a*) " Grace "—that aid from GOD that Paul himself had found always " sufficient ", II Corinthians xii. 9, the great life-changer, " what I am ", and life-charger, " I laboured " of I Corinthians xv. 10. Such is the always adequate secret whose fulness will ever be at Timothy's disposal. And at ours ! Why, then, should we ever fail, in character or in conduct ? (*b*) " Mercy "—that GOD will mercifully secure for him that he shall never be over-awed by the power of the enemy, never over-driven by the pressure of circumstances, never over-strained by the problems of the task, never over-weighted by the perils of the way. After all, as Paul knew so well, " GOD is faithful [as well as merciful], who will not suffer you to be tempted above that ye are able . . .", 1 Corinthians x. 13. We may all rest upon the assurance that His merciful provision and protection will be available as we set forth upon His service. (*c*) " Peace "—how precious a boon. The ocean may, in its depths, be still and quiet, even though its surface be storm-tossed. It is not just outward peacefulness that is open to Christians ; but this persistent peace which, to normal thinking, is so extraordinary, this " peace of GOD which passeth all understanding ", of which this same Paul writes, in Philippians iv. 7, this " My peace " of the Saviour, in John xiv. 27, which not even the cruel circumstances of His outward experience could disturb. " Grace, mercy, and peace "—such are the blessings that Paul craves for Timothy, that the fact of them, the reality of them, the experience of them, may be his inner strength and stay, however trying, and even turbulent, the outward conditions may be. Speaking of this latter—

PAUL INDICATES THE DIFFICULTIES AHEAD

Here we are, then, with our attention concentrated on (i) *The Ephesian Church*—" at Ephesus ", verse 3. That company of true believers had been begun through the work of Paul, and was furthered and fostered probably by the apostle John, and by such other teachers as Apollos and Aquila and Priscilla. Paul devoted a good deal of care to, and had a real affection for, these Ephesians. He paid them a brief visit at the end of his Second

Missionary Tour, Acts xviii. 19 ; at the outset of his Third Journey he spent no less than three years with them, Acts xix. 1 ; xx. 31. On his last visit to Jerusalem, he stopped awhile at a seaside town, thirty miles from Ephesus, that the church leaders from the great city might run down for a farewell meeting with him, Acts xx. 17—a most affecting occasion, as verses 36–8 show. The mother church at Ephesus, and the daughter churches of the district, seem to have made good and rapid progress in the spiritual life, if we may judge by the high level of the doctrine that Paul felt able to address to them in the circular letter described in our Bibles as to the Ephesians. In the two oldest MSS. the words " at Ephesus ", i. 1, are omitted, which suggests that the blank space was, in the original, left to be filled in with the names of the various churches in the group. Most of the modern scholars hold this view nowadays. The supporting internal evidence for this opinion is helpfully, and I think convincingly, summed up by Dr. Graham Scroggie in his invaluable *Know Your Bible*, Vol. II. It is to these local churches that Paul is led to reveal the " mystery " of the Church, in this Epistle, to quote Dr. Scroggie, " in struggling terms, that is, in language which struggles to express the inexpressible " ; and again, " In Ephesians, Church truth blazes forth in fulness of glory ". All which has encouraged me to hazard the guess that the Christians in this area had reached a high level of spiritual understanding and experience. How sad it is, then, to read the record of their fall, within the century, in Revelation ii. 4, " Nevertheless I have somewhat against thee, because thou hast left thy first love ". Well, dear reader, what about your local church ? And what about yourself as one of its members ? As the American jingle ran—

> " What sort of a church would my church be,
>   If every church member were just like me ? "

And what is to be said of (ii) *The Ephesian Church Business*. It is hinted at, by implication, in our passage. (*a*) " That they teach [the] doctrine ", verse 3. Because " other " doctrine was projected, true doctrine must be proclaimed : the doctrine of full and free salvation by faith in the Saviour alone. And, by the way, it is interesting and instructive to read, in Acts xx. 21, Paul's own account of what his doctrine of man's part in salvation had been, in his Ephesian ministry, " Testifying both to the Jews, and also to the Greeks, repentance toward GOD, and faith toward our

Lord JESUS CHRIST ". How often we present-day preachers, in our eagerness to emphasise the necessity of the " faith ", tend to omit, or obscure, the need also for the " repentance ". This doctrine of salvation, then, and all other Scriptural doctrine, in its purity and beauty, is to be taught to men, as part of the " glorious gospel ", verse 11, that we shall consider in our next study. Because the devil makes it his business to see that false teaching is spread abroad, it becomes the Church's urgent business to make sure of the dissemination of the good seed of the Word. And so to secure (b) " Godly edifying which is in faith ", verse 4. Let it not, in these loosely taught days, be forgotten that the feeding with " sound doctrine ", verse 10, is the sole but sure means of building up in the faith those who have come to put their trust in CHRIST. I am personally of the opinion that one of the causes of weakness in the churches to-day is the virtual disappearance from our pulpits of sound, steady, Scriptural, expository teaching, and that a widespread return to that desirable practice is essential to the solid building-up of our members in the faith. Here then are two fundamental items in the business of any church, or of its leaders—educating and edifying, and the two are really one. There are many other things that it is the church's business to do ; but it is these particular duties that were incumbent upon the Ephesian teachers, and upon Timothy, who was to preside over them.

That leads us on to consider (iii) *The Ephesian Church Dangers.* There were perils enough in the world around, with all the evils inevitably associated with the heathen atmosphere in which these newborn Christians had now to live. Some of us do not know what this sort of thing means, what it means for native converts, or, for that matter, what it means for still-human missionaries, to live and work under the dead weight and living menace of pagan surroundings. Let us not forget to pray for our missionaries in this regard, and for the converts, too, who have but lately come out of vile heathendom. Ephesus was given up to the fanatical and frenzied worship of " the great goddess Diana ", Acts xix. 27. Yet, more perilous still were the dangers arising from the false teaching being promulgated within church circles. It is this that young Timothy will have by reason of his new position to deal with—and that Paul would forewarn him of and prepare him for. This (a) " Other doctrine " —creeping into the church, so different from what they had been taught of the pure gospel. Whatever new and fresh truth GOD has to bring to man, it will never be anything that is contrary to

His revealed word and will in the Scriptures. There is our undeviating touchstone of truth. These (b) "Fables", Dr. David Smith has said that, "In those early days when as yet there were no written Gospels . . . it was easy for the heretics to gain credence for their doctrines by inventing fables regarding Him". Some of the fantastic stories of His childhood for instance, that are still extant, are evidence enough of this sorry traffic. Those (c) "Endless genealogies". Some would refer these to the incipient beginnings of that troublous teaching so prevalent later which, founded upon the supposed inherent evil of matter, said that the all-holy Deity could have no direct touch with it, and therefore could not have Himself actually created the physical, or material, world, and that it necessitated a succession of lessening æons in genealogical sequence till one appeared less holy enough to handle the earth's construction. Dean Alford is inclined to accept this interpretation, though he is careful to state " not the full-blown Gnosticism (as it was called) of the second century ", but some primal early form of it. Others, however, would see in these " genealogies " a certain Jewish element of which examples are to be found in the Talmud. Dr. E. F. Scott, in the *Moffatt Commentary*, says, " The lists of bare names in Old Testament genealogies were easily expanded into fictitious histories, supposed to illustrate God's dealings with His people. . . . The practice, indeed, was so common that the word ' genealogy ' was often used in the sense of mythical history, and this would seem to be its meaning in the present verse." These fictions were " endless "—there was no end to them ; and the effect of these interminable stories was only to " minister questions "—to arouse speculation and argument and controversy instead of contributing to the proper sturdiness of Christian faith.

So there it is. When " Youth Takes the Helm ", he will find himself beset with difficulties and dangers moral, spiritual, and even physical—for tradition has it that this young bishop was eventually beaten to death in Ephesus. However, at the outset, to be forewarned was to be forearmed ; and this Epistle will guide and cheer him as he takes up his very responsible task.

I had originally entitled this book, " Youth Takes the Helm ", which does represent the situation envisaged in the Epistle; but as there is another book on the market bearing that title, I was advised to suggest another name—which I have done.

II

MALADY AND REMEDY

I TIMOTHY i. 5–11

5 Now the end of the commandment is charity out of a pure heart, and *of* a good conscience, and *of* faith unfeigned :

6 From which some having swerved have turned aside unto vain jangling ;

7 Desiring to be teachers of the law ; understanding neither what they say, nor whereof they affirm.

8 But we know that the law *is* good, if a man use it lawfully ;

9 Knowing this, that the law is not made for a righteous man, but for the lawless and disobedient, for the ungodly and for sinners, for unholy and profane, for murderers of fathers and murderers of mothers, for manslayers.

10 For whoremongers, for them that defile themselves with mankind, for menstealers, for liars, for perjured persons, and if there be any other thing that is contrary to sound doctrine ;

11 According to the glorious gospel of the blessed God, which was committed to my trust.

THE passage really begins further back than our Title suggests, for a glance at verse 5 shows us—

A PICTURE OF GOOD HEALTH

Just look at the marks of it that are there apparent. (i) " *Unfeigned Faith.*" The real thing. There is of course a spurious faith ; there is a misplaced faith ; there is a so-called faith which consists only in the mental acceptance of a doctrine, or in the mere recital of a creed. Mental acceptance is of course, so far as it goes, a good thing ; but it does not carry us far enough. James ii. 19 is sufficient to show us that : " Thou believest that there is one GOD ; thou doest well : the devils also believe . . ." The apostle here means something more than this—not merely the belief *about* Him, acknowledging His historicity ; nor merely the belief *in* Him, acknowledging His ability ; but the belief *on* Him, resting on His saving quality—as in Acts xvi. 31, for instance, or John iii. 16, Gk., or a score of other passages. It is that same " unfeigned faith " which Timothy himself possessed,

following the example of mother and grandmother, II Timothy
i. 5. Have we this faith ? And how much of it have we ? " Oh
thou of little faith ", says the Master in Matthew xiv. 31, of His
disciple ; and in the very next chapter, xv. 28, " O woman,
great is thy faith ". Are we amongst the Littles ; or do we
belong to the Greats ? Anyhow, if our faith, however small to
begin with, is of the real sort, it is bound to grow, with exercise,
bigger and stronger.

Note another mark of the truly healthy Christian, (ii) " *Good
Conscience* ". A consciousness of freedom from guilt, as on the
manward side, and as on the Godward side. A thankful, grateful
realisation that there is nothing to spoil our fellowship, either
with Him—or with them. Paul had said earlier to Felix, in Acts
xxiv. 16 ; " I exercise myself [took earnest pains to secure it] to
have always a conscience void of offence toward GOD, and toward
men ". Of course, though we be conscious of " nothing between ",
as Evan Hopkins' convention hymn expresses it, it does not follow
that there is nothing amiss down in the sub-consciousness, which
the convicting light of the HOLY SPIRIT may later bring out,
to be put right. This is, I imagine, what Paul means when he
writes in I Corinthians iv. 4, " I know nothing [that is, to be
wrong] by myself ; yet am I not hereby justified : but He that
judgeth me is the LORD." He may see things that, as yet, I
do not see—I may pass man's judgment, I may pass self-judg-
ment, but how does He judge of me ? If at any time He reveal
anything amiss, let us fly at once to Him—and to any whom
He shows us to have wronged—and get clear of it. How priceless
a boon it is to have a sensitive conscience.

Another health rule is a (iii) " *Pure Heart* ". Here we get
down to the depth of us, and we are faced with the matter of
motive. Why did we say, why did we do, that kind thing ?
Honestly now, was it that we might be thought well of ? Or
was it that we expected, or at least hoped, to get something
out of it—that " a recompense be made thee ", as our Lord
devastatingly warns us, in Luke xiv. 12 ? Or was it out of sheer
goodness of heart, out of real sympathy, out of a sincere desire
to be a help ? Let us never obscure the fact that the more important thing is, not what we do, but why we do it. Why did
that medical man go so regularly to church ? Not because he
desired the worship of GOD, but because he conceived the idea
that it would make him *persona grata* with the well-to-do congregation, and so secure for him the building up of a good practice.
Let me hasten to add that this is not the sorry case with all medical

churchmen. It is only intended as a stricture upon one particular physician that I once knew. Here, again, is one particular grocer, meticulously careful about weights and measures—not because of inner rectitude, but only because of inner fear, lest any departure from exactitude should land him in trouble. Oh yes, *what* is important,; but not so important as *why*. In this connection as in· so many others it is well to remember that while " man looketh on the outward appearance . . . the LORD looketh on the heart ", I Sámuel xvi. 7. What a good thing it is to have a pure heart—an inner being released from all selfish and unworthy motives.

Highest evidence of spiritual health, of course, is (iv) "Charity". An originally lovely word that has, alas, gathered to itself an ugly connotation ; and whose present substitute is Love—not the " Eros ", which is but unholy desire, and has no right to the use of the name Love, and which is not found in the New Testament ; and not the " Philo ", or " Phileo ", which represent simply natural affection, and which was as far as poor Peter felt he could go in the post-resurrection interview with the LORD, John xxi. 15–17 ; but the " Agape ", which is the Divine gift, " the love of GOD is shed abroad in our hearts by the HOLY GHOST who is given unto us ", Romans v. 5. It is no overstatement or mis-statement to say that this is an infallible thermometer, revealing the normal temperature, or the low temperature, of the Christian. Is there real love in our hearts ? If so, it is a sure sign that we are in good spiritual health ; if not, we are assuredly suffering from very poor health—and to think that we could possess this quality as our Romans quotation directs !

In verse 3 we learnt that Paul laid a " charge " upon young Timothy, that he was to combat, and to counteract, certain false doctrine—of which, more presently. In this verse 5, the word translated " commandment " is the same as that rendered " charge ". Paul therefore is here saying that the " end ", or aim, of the charge is love. In executing this that is enjoined upon him, the young bishop will sometimes have to take stringent action, will sometimes by way of command or of controversy have to say some very straight things ; but he is exhorted to remember always to act, and to speak, in a spirit of love— " speaking the truth in love ", says Paul in another Epistle, Ephesians iv. 15. The first three words are but one in the Greek —truthing [it] in love. Moffatt renders it, " hold by the truth in love " ; Armitage Robinson has " maintaining the truth in

love " ; Alford gives us, " followers of truth in love " ; **and**
Handley Moule comments, " It certainly means more than truth-
speaking."   It is so easy, when loyalty to the truth compels us
to engage in controversy, or to take sides, to speak or act harshly
and haughtily ; whereas the reader of this Letter is counselled
that in his attitude all is to be characterised by love.   The
" end " of the charge is not to win the argument but to win
the man ; and let those whose nimble wits have given them the
doubly dangerous gift of repartee remember that to score off
your man may be to scare him from the truth.   Well—what a
fine healthy Christian is here depicted in the display of the three
last qualities, " out of " which, as the supreme test, emerges the
characteristic of love.   But now, verses 6–10 remind us of—

The People in Bad Health

" From which [spiritual soundness] some having swerved have
turned aside into vain jangling." As Dr. F. E. Scott puts it,
" Like travellers who leave the high road for a path that leads
nowhere. . . . This byway is described as empty argument, or
vain chatter." What, then, was the matter with these people,
what was their malady ? Paul, like the specialist that he is,
comes to the aid of Timothy, the general practitioner, in helping
him with the diagnosis before going on to prescribe the treatment.
Two symptoms are noted, very closely related to each other :
the first is so often followed by the other. That first is (i) *Wrong
Doctrine.* Some " other doctrine ", verse 3, than that which they
had at the beginning been taught ; something to do with
" the law ", verse 7. Now of course (*a*) The law is bad if it is in
the wrong place. That is one of the major themes of Galatians
and of Romans ; and these for whom Timothy is responsible
are " desiring to be teachers of the law " instead of the Gospel ;
preceptors of law rather than of grace ; and not even using the
law legitimately, but abusing it—as Alford says, they " founded
on Judaism . . . idle fables and allegories [see our verse 4 again],
letting in latitude of morals and unholiness of life ". Not that
they really understood what they were saying or what they were
talking about—their speech and their subject were alike un-
intelligible even to themselves. Fine sort of teachers ! On the
other hand " we know ", verse 8, that (*b*) The law is good if it is
in its right place—if it is put and kept to its " lawful " use. We
turn instinctively to that illuminating statement in Galatians
iii. 24, " The law was our schoolmaster to bring us to Christ ".

Three lessons taught us by this " pedagogue " are used to drive us to the Saviour. First Lesson : We ought—the standard at whose level we should be living. Second Lesson : We haven't —never for a single moment have we come up to GOD's ideal of conduct. Third Lesson : We can't—we just are not able to reach the standard. Which three lessons teach us, in the words of Dr. A. T. Pierson's hymn, " How helpless and hopeless we sinners had been ", if GOD had not of His infinite mercy and sovereign grace provided a way by which " we might be justified by faith ". Verily, then, " the law is good ", if it be thus allowed to exercise its salutary ministry of conviction of our true state and our great need. Indeed in verses 9–10 we shall see Paul using it in this very way.

For we turn now to consider the second symptom of this people's ill condition, (ii) *Wrong Doing*. How often, as we have said, doctrine and doing go together—whether the good, or the bad. A world-famous evangelist went so far as to say that of the supposedly intellectual difficulties that were brought to him almost all turned out to be moral. A more recent scholar, Dr. Scott, of New York, has said, " More often than we know, religious error has its roots in moral rather than in intellectual causes." Certainly it can scarcely be gainsaid that by and large and in the long run there is an intimate connection between what a man believes and what a man is. Do you remember how Proverbs xxiii. 7 puts it—" as he thinketh in his heart, so is he ". We have been considering these people's wrong doctrine : I am not surprised that Paul feels impelled to go on to point out their wrong doing. And how strikingly he shows it—by the proper use of " the law ", in verses 9–10. Taking up the great Ten Words of the universal Moral Law, he deals, to begin with, with (a) The First Table, our duty towards GOD—about (1) No other GOD. (2) No graven image. (3) No profaning the Name. (4) No forgetting the holy Day. In the light of these demands, Paul shows those who are convicted of being lawless and disobedient, ungodly and sinners, unholy and profane. When he comes to (b) The Second Table, our duty towards our Neighbour, he speaks with greater particularity, choosing the more excessive instances of each violation, (5) Father and mother—" murderers of fathers and murderers of mothers ". (6) Murder—" manslayers ". (7) Adultery—" whoremongers, and them that defile themselves with mankind. (8) Stealing—" menstealers ", taking into forced slavery. (9) False witness—" liars and perjured persons ". (10) **Covet, anything that is his**—" any other thing that is contrary ".

So by this lawful use of the Law as a convicting medium does this apostle show up the wrong-doing of those concerned. It is a woeful demonstration of the low state of moral health to which many have sunk, whom Timothy, like many a bishop or presbyter since, will have to meet, a situation which he will have to seek grace and power to tackle. Thank GOD, he is in possession of—

THE PRESCRIPTION FOR RENEWED HEALTH

" The glorious gospel of the blessed GOD, which was committed to my trust ", verse 11. Here is, indeed, the sovereign remedy of the world's ill, and of the soul's sickness. But notice first that phrase at the end of verse 10, " sound doctrine ", healthy teaching. In a day when quack nostrums abound, when spurious medicines parade our streets and come knocking at our doors, it is well to know of this " sound " prescription, compounded of guaranteed ingredients from the Bible Pharmacœpia, a soul's medicament which not only is " sound " in itself, but which engenders soundness in those who trust and take it. How delightful is the description, in Luke xv. 27, of the returned prodigal—" safe and sound ". May we all have right to both adjectives. It can only be so from our partaking of (i) *The Complete Cure*—" the glorious gospel ". Too often, and too long, some of us have imagined that the gospel is restricted to making us " safe "—saving us from the guilt, and doom, and stain, and habit, and power of sin. Thank GOD, it has that enormous effect, and we can never be too thankful for all that ; but let us never forget that the gospel has also, and is intended to have, a positive effect, as well as the negative result. It is calculated to make us " sound "—not only Christians, but healthy Christians. As our Church of England Collect for St. Luke's Day prays, " May it please Thee, that, by the wholesome medicines of the doctrine delivered by him, all the diseases of our souls may be healed ". " The glorious gospel "—it is, indeed, " good tidings ", Luke ii. 10, glorious news for the sons of men ; but the Revised Version renders the phrase, " the gospel of the Glory " ; and that, too, is beautifully true. The research chemists of the soul could never have found this healing stream ; it is an Essence distilled in the Glory, and sent down here to " be of sin the double cure " —negative and positive ; as well as " from its guilt and power ", as Toplady's hymn reminds us. Not only does it come down from the Glory, but it also takes us up to the Glory, in its own miraculous way it fits us for the Glory, so that, in the Great Day, and in a sense different from, and deeper than, that of the parable, it shall be said of each true believer, " Thy [heavenly] Father hath received him safe and sound "—and there will be no cantankerous and self-righteous " brother " then to spoil the Joy of the Homecoming. We see, therefore, that it is because it is a gospel of the Glory that it is such a glorious gospel.

We continue in that same theme as we think of (ii) *The Wondrous Source*—" of the blessed GOD ". It is permissible to apply to the Gospel the words originally written of its amazing outcome, the New Birth, in John i. 13, that it is, " not of blood "—of inherited gift ; " nor of the will of the flesh "—of our own fleshly effort ; " nor of the will of man "—of any other man's urging ; " but of GOD "—we say again, and can never say too often, He is the Divine Author and Source of the Gospel of our Salvation. He is here described as " the blessed GOD " ; but the late Dr. Campbell Morgan, in his *Searchlights from the Word*, encourages us in rendering the description as " the happy GOD ". Certainly, the Greek word will bear that interpretation ; and if the association of that quality of happiness with the Deity be held to be somewhat irreverent, and even flippant, it should be sufficient, by way of answer, to recall how frequently the idea is found in relation to the Second Divine Person of the Holy Trinity. He Himself speaks of " My joy ", even in the threatening circumstances of the Upper Room, with Gethsemane, Gabbatha, and Golgotha in the immediate future, John xv. 11 ; His personal Return is described as " that [happy] Hope ", Titus ii. 13 ; and it is said of Him that " Thy GOD hath anointed Thee with the oil of gladness above Thy fellows ", Hebrews i. 9. Moreover, time after time, in the Old Testament, we have the conception of a rejoicing GOD. For example, " As the bridegroom rejoiceth over the bride, so shall thy GOD rejoice over thee ", Isaiah lxii. 5 ; and " The LORD thy GOD . . . will rejoice over thee with joy. . . . He will joy over thee with singing ", Zephaniah iii. 17. We do not wonder that Bishop Bernard said, " GOD is not only the Object of His creatures' blessing, but has in Himself the fulness of bliss ". In answering his own propounded question, " Do we wish for the real happiness that GOD enjoys ? " Dr. Eugene Stock pointed to the fact that the Beatitudes of Matthew v. all begin with this same Greek word for " Happy " ! This " glorious gospel ", this gospel of the Glory, comes, indeed, out of an environment of joy, out of the happy Heart of GOD. It is not, therefore, to be wondered at that it brings such happiness to the heart of the man that accepts it. No, not so much " it ", as " Him " ; for, in the long run, the Gospel is GOD, just as Christianity is CHRIST.

Consider, finally, (iii) *The Grave Responsibility*—" which was committed to my trust ". We have been considering our present passage under a medical simile—Malady and Remedy. It will not come amiss, therefore, if I remind you of a very delightful practice that obtains in the profession, that if any one of them, by some research, makes a discovery that may benefit mankind, he will not keep it to himself, but will publish it abroad, in the pages of *The Lancet*, perhaps, or through some other channel, where it can be thoroughly ventilated and discussed, and so contribute to the easing of man's ills. That is one difference between the " quack " and the genuine practitioner ; the former will keep any secret he may stumble upon to himself, that he may accumulate gain to his own pocket. I am reminded of that grand story in the Old Testament, of the four leprous men, outside the besieged city of Samaria, discussing their miserable plight. To seek entrance to the city will mean death, for there is no food there ; to stay where they are will mean death, for there is no food there either ; to go to the camp of the besieging army of the Syrians seems the only course open to them—if the soldiers kill them, they will but die, which they will do if they stay ; and perchance they will take pity on them. If ever men were on the horns of a dilemma, it is these four people. They decided to risk it ; and to their amazement, for a reason that the Bible story explains, they found the Syrians had fled, leaving their camp intact. We can imagine with what glee and gluttony they fell upon the food. In the midst of it all, a sudden thought disturbed them ; they recollected the starving thousands shut up in the city—perishing for dire need of the supplies that were so near at hand. One of the lepers voiced what was the feeling of them all, " We do not well : this day is a day of good tidings, and we hold our peace ", II Kings vii. 9. Ours too is a gospel day : thousands, yea millions, are starving for the Bread of Life, upon whom we have fed and feasted our souls. Are we doing " well ", or ill ? Are we publishing the good news abroad, or are we—out of selfishness, shyness, or slothfulness—keeping the glad secret to ourselves ? Paul is keenly aware that " the glorious gospel " is not merely for his own salvation and enjoyment, but has been committed to him as a trust for the eternal benefit of others. It was that compelling sense of trusteeship that led him to the endurance of such sufferings. Read II Corinthians xi. 23-7

again to see what this intrepid man suffered in discharge of his
" trust ". Yet, he could look at it only as a privilege—" we were
allowed of GOD to be put in trust with the gospel ", he writes,
in I Thessalonians ii. 4. We must, of course, not forget that there
was another, and even stronger, element in the deep urge to
propagate the gospel. Paul tells us about it in II Corinthians
v. 14, " The love of CHRIST constraineth us ". The need of men
—the sense of trust—the love of CHRIST : what a trinity of
impelling motive-power ! It is the second that Paul is here
concerned to impress on Timothy at this point. He has been
shown the Remedy for man's Malady—he has taken the Healing
Medicine for himself ; and now he must be ever eager to let
others know about it ; and the Ephesian Church must also be
assiduous in publishing it. Any church that lacks the missionary
spirit is in grave danger of losing its own spiritual health—as the
North African Church, founded, perhaps, through the testimony
of the Ethiopian Chancellor, of Acts viii. 27, discovered to its
undoing, for it failed apparently in its gospel trusteeship. A
church, a Christian, that persistently takes in without giving
out, becomes eventually, and inevitably, a Dead Sea ! Let us
all take that seriously, and solemnly, to heart.

III

PERSECUTOR BECOME PREACHER

I Timothy i. 12–17

12 And I thank Christ Jesus our Lord, who hath enabled me, for that he counted me faithful, putting me into the ministry ;

13 Who was before a blasphemer, and a persecutor, and injurious : but I obtained mercy, because I did *it* ignorantly in unbelief.

14 And the grace of our Lord was exceeding abundant with faith and love which is in Christ Jesus.

15 This *is* a faithful saying, and worthy of all acceptation, that Christ Jesus came into the world to save sinners ; of whom I am chief.

16 Howbeit for this cause I obtained mercy, that in me first Jesus Christ might shew forth all longsuffering, for a pattern to them which should hereafter believe on him to life everlasting.

17 Now unto the King eternal, immortal, invisible, the only wise God, *be* honour and glory for ever and ever. Amen.

WE recall that Paul is writing to give Timothy all the help, guidance, and inspiration that he can on his taking up his responsible office. The apostle realises that as this young friend of his assumes the Oversight he will be brought up against all kinds of problems, and will be confronted by seemingly inflexible, and certainly intimidating, opposition. He would like Timothy to be quite sure in his own mind that even the toughest foe can be brought low by the convicting and conquering power and love of the living CHRIST, whose ambassador he is. Can Paul think of the story of any such conquest, that would bring encouragement to the young evangelist ? Indeed he can : he will tell him his own story ! A story so remarkable that people could scarcely believe it to be true. The loyal disciple, Ananias, says, " I have heard by many of this man, how much evil he hath done to Thy saints ", Acts ix. 13—it takes a special reassurance from the Lord Himself to convince him of the sincerity of this Saul's conversion, believing at first that the persecutor was setting a trap to catch him in avowing his Christian discipleship. The believers at Jerusalem " were all afraid of him, and believed not that he was a disciple ", Acts ix. 26—it took all the guarantee of the beloved Barnabas to persuade them that his conversion was genuine. It was some time before it dawned upon the churches of Judæa at last that it really was the delightfully delirious fact " that he which persecuted us in times past now preacheth the faith which once he destroyed ", Galatians i. 23. Yes, Timothy, you will never come across a harder case, or a greater triumph : if GOD can save Saul, He can save anyone you will come up against in Ephesus. And all because, in another sense, of—

A TRUE STORY

Look at our verse 15, " This is a faithful saying, and worthy of all acceptation, that CHRIST JESUS came into the world to save sinners ". We call to mind the glorious stories of Sir Walter Scott, Robert Louis Stevenson, Bulwer Lytton, Fenimore Cooper, Henry Seton Merriman, Anthony Trollope, Joseph Conrad, Baroness Orczy, John Buchan—what a galaxy of tale-bearers ; but never, never, in all the world was a story like this which Paul would have Timothy pass on far and wide. (i) *A Mystery Story*—" CHRIST JESUS came into the world ". If it had been said that JESUS came into the world, there would have been no mystery about that, for many bearing that name had come into the world. It was a quite common name. Origen tells us that it was the name of Barabbas—that latter being only his description : Son of the father, Son of the Rabbi, Son of the manse ? How vivid, then, is Pilate's enquiry, " Whom will ye that I release unto you ? Barabbas, or JESUS which is called CHRIST ? " Matthew xxvii. 17. Which JESUS will you have ? A common name ; but how exquisitely rare it has become, now that the Saviour bore it. Old Dr. Johnson said of Oliver Goldsmith that " he touched nothing that he did not adorn " : how infinitely more true of our Lord, who invested with glory a common city, a common work, a common cross, a common name. Yes ; but what made the mystery was its connection with that other name, CHRIST—the anointed One, the holy One, the heavenly One, the promised Messiah. Here the Human and the Divine meet in One. The GOD-man appears on the earth, " came into the world "—truly human, as truly Divine ; truly Divine, as truly human. Beyond explanation, of human reason ; but not beyond experience, through Divine grace. How we thank GOD for the Humanity, for the Deity, for the Trinity in Unity.

Leaving that very poorly expressed side of the matter, we see here, next, (ii) *An Adventure Story*—" to save sinners ". In Luke xix. 10, the Master Himself put it, " The Son of man is come to seek and to save that which was lost ". We reverently think of Him as He embarks upon that long-planned Errand of Rescue, (a) Leaving the Glory. Can you not imagine the scene as the multitude of angels gather about the heavenly gates to speed Him on His way ? Though He voluntarily embarked upon the task, yet He was so often telling us that He was " sent " upon the great adventure by the Father, e.g., John iv. 34 ; v. 37 ; vi. 44 ; vii. 33 ; xvii. 18, etc. And how eagerly those angels we just mentioned watched Him down here (b) Living the Life— the Lord of Glory mingling with the sinful sons of men, the " Friend of publicans and sinners ", Luke vii. 34. How greatly privileged some of the heavenly ones felt at being sent to His aid in times of His special stress and strain, as in the Wilderness, Matthew iv. 11, and in the Garden, Luke xxii. 43. Ah, it was a costly business, this search for precious souls, this (c) Loving the sheep—knowing their danger, hearing their cry, following their track, rescuing their souls, bringing them home, the Good Shepherd, not merely risking His life, but giving His life for the sheep, John x. 11. How those angels watched ; and how merrily their music rang out when, one by one, the crowns of the Great Adventure were heralded in the skies, Luke xv. 7, 10.

None of us will fail to see this as (iii) *A Love Story*. Why should the Almighty bother about the Atom ? Only for one over-mastering reason : in spite of our insignificance, " when we were yet without strength " ; in spite of our wrong-doing, " while we were yet sinners " ; in spite of our rebellion, " when we were enemies ", His heart was set upon us. " GOD commendeth His love toward us, in that, while we were yet sinners, CHRIST died for us ", Romans v. 6, 8, 10. Again we ask, why should the All-holy be ready to pay such a price to redeem the All-sinful ? Only love can account for it—amazing love. Do you remember the lines of E. C. Clephane's hymn—

> " Two wonders I confess—
> The wonders of His glorious love,
> And my own worthlessness."

Let it be emphasised, then, with uttermost gratitude, that this is (iv) *A True Story*. The apostle has piled up the words to ram that fact home—" this is a faithful saying, and worthy of all acceptation ". It is no fancy of a disordered imagination, no figment of a distraught emotionalism ; it is known to be true in the experience both of Paul and of Timothy, shown to be true in the case of every real believer since. Can you, my reader, not add your own " Amen " to that affirmation ? Has not this CHRIST JESUS saved you, as He came into the world to do ? Was there ever a story like this—of such wide appeal, of such vast circulation, of such engrossing interest, of such compelling power ?

It is interesting to observe that, in the pastoral epistles—and they occur nowhere else—there are five of these " faithful sayings ", or " trewe words ", as John Wycliffe describes them : (1) Concerning our Life's Salvation, here, in I Timothy i. 15. (2) Concerning our Life's Service, in I Timothy iii. 1.   (3) Concerning our Life's Suffering, in I Timothy iv. 9–10.   (4) Concerning our Life's Sanctification, in Titus iii. 8.   (5) Concerning our Life's Secret, in II Timothy ii. 11.   Professor David Smith, in his Disciple's Commentary, has the interesting suggestion that, in these " logia ", Paul is quoting from a manual that Luke had drawn up for the guidance of teachers and pastors—maxims, watchwords, epitomes of truth, " coin current stamped with the superscription which marked them as coming from the true mint of GOD ", as T. A. Gurney puts it.   And now we turn from what we may call the theoretical side of the matter to its more personal and practical aspect as we consider—

A GOOD SPECIMEN

When, in young days, we were presented with a story-book, it was always the pictures that attracted us first, and most.   And, in speaking of the wonder of saving grace and power, Paul offers himself as an outstanding illustration of it.

Not that he felt that he had, in any sense, deserved it.   How readily he would have joined in the lines of the century-old hymn—

> " Jesu, what didst Thou find in me
> That Thou hast dealt so lovingly ? "

His explanation is, (i) " *I obtained mercy* ", verse 13.   That is How it was.   He was the object of (a) Emancipating Grace.   Till then he had been " a blasphemer, and a persecutor, and injurious " —how always humbled he was at the recollection of the sordid story.   There was just this one atom of palliation, that " I did it ignorantly ".   But, who is this that talks of ignorance ?   This is one of the most brilliant brains of his time, one of the most famous products of his university of Tarsus, one of the most noteworthy of the pupils of that scholar and professor of world-wide reputation, the Jowett of Balliol of his day, Gamaliel of Jerusalem. This Saul was the fortunate possessor of an intellectual equipment second to none. Ignorance is a word that sounds strangely in relation to such a man. Ah yes—but there is a realm of knowledge whose doors are fast barred against natural gifts, however eminent, for " the natural man receiveth not the things of the SPIRIT of GOD, for they are foolishness unto him, neither can he know them, because they are spiritually discerned ", I Corinthians ii. 14. We are infinitely distressed, but we need not be disturbed, by the statements of our Russells, our Haldanes, our Huxleys, on religious, spiritual, Biblical, Christian things—for all their magnificent learning in their own spheres, they are here completely out of their depth. They just don't know : neither did Saul—till that never-to-be-forgotten occasion when, by the blinding light above that of the noontide sun, he saw the light of the truth as it is in the living Lord JESUS, when the closing of his outward vision was the prelude to his inward sight. Then it was that GOD delivered him " from so great a death ", II Corinthians i. 10, and " from the power of darkness " and " translated [him] into the kingdom of His dear Son ", Colossians i. 13. Thenceforward he was a gloriously emancipated man. Then there was (b) Employing Grace. " He counted me faithful, putting me into the ministry." Be it noted that emancipation is never an end in itself, but always a means to an end, always with a view to employment—salvation is to be followed by service. How grandly so in Paul's case. In whatever sort of work we are employed for Him, it is always to be a " ministry of reconciliation ", in the sense of II Corinthians v. 18–19. God had counted him " faithful "—that is, trustworthy ; and so He had trusted him with this blessed ministry. May He find us also to be as those that He can rely on to do whatever service He may, in His wisdom and grace, appoint us. Here, too, is (c) Enabling Grace. " Who hath enabled me." Let no timid, or hesitant Christian hold back from service from a sense of in-sufficiency—truly, " our sufficiency is of GOD ", II Corinthians iii. 5. Never does He bid us go upon His errands without supplying us with all we need for the discharging of the commission ; never does He send us to engage the foe without providing us with all the accoutrement and equipment that we require for the battle and the victory—" who goeth a warfare at his own charges ? " says I Corinthians ix. 7. Let the earnest believer take comfort and courage from the plain statement of Exodus xviii. 23, " If

God command thee . . . thou shalt be able to . . ." It is in this sense that Augustine said, " Give what Thou commandest; then, command what Thou wilt ". One other thought is here, that of (d) Exceeding Grace. " The grace of the LORD was exceeding abundant " Huperepleonasen. Paul is fond of compound words with " huper " : one is tempted to render it, in accordance with schoolboy slang, as " super " ! And, indeed, His grace would need to be of such a quality in order to meet the condition of this apostle, who describes himself, here, in verse 15, as " chief " of sinners. This is no exaggeration, as all will know who have ever come under the deep convicting power of the HOLY SPIRIT. The young prophet of Isaiah vi. 5 knew it when the cry was wrought from him, " Woe is me, for I am undone ". The disciple of Luke v. 8 knew it when he besought, " Depart from me, for I am a sinful man ". The publican of Luke xviii. 13 understood it when, in uttermost contrition, he confessed, " GOD be merciful to me _the_ sinner ", Gk.—not " a ", but " the ", as if, in comparison with the outwardly righteous Pharisee ; or, more likely, " the ", as if, at that moment, he felt as if he were the only sinner there ! So this Paul cannot get away from the thought that, but for the exceeding grace, his wickedness was the all-sufficient cause of his worthlessness—" not meet to be called an apostle ", I Corinthians xv. 9 ; " less than the least of all saints ", Ephesians iii. 8. Yet, grace made him what he was, and enabled him to work as he did —" but by the grace of GOD I am what I am : and His grace . . . was not in vain, but I laboured more abundantly than they all : yet not I, but the grace of GOD which was with me ", I Corinthians xv. 10. Ah yes, merciful and mighty was that grace, leading him on to that " faith and love ", verse 14, which he thenceforward exhibited in such abundant measure towards the CHRIST JESUS to whom previously he had displayed such unbelief and hate.

We turn to that other use of the phrase (ii) " _I obtained mercy_ ", in verse 16. That is why it was. He was the gladly privileged recipient of all this mercy in order that He might be " a pattern " of His long suffering and tender dealing, (a) That all might enjoy —this is not Paul's exclusive prerogative. " In me first ", it is true ; but not in me only. The apostle's whole subsequent life was devoted to the proclamation that the Calvary dealing with sin was " not for ours only ", I John ii. 2—he longed that others should hear the grand news. Paul's blessing is ours too. (b) That none need despair—if GOD could do this for such an one as this persecuting and pernicious fellow, verse 13, then truly all could hope. If a man like Paul could be so gloriously saved, then so could any man, however bad he might be—that is a vital principle of the apostle's philosophy of salvation : none is too bad for redeeming grace. He is himself a conspicuous specimen of that truth. And so to—

A FINE SEQUEL

In former days one often read upon the title-page of a book that the story, " So and So " was a sequel to the tale, " Such and Such ". Thus it may be said that verse 17 is the outcome of verse 15, that the True Story of the earlier paragraph is followed by the Fine Sequel of this latter. It all seems so proper that it should be so. As T. A. Gurney says, " We almost expect this doxology in the place where we find it ". It will be not untrue to say that a doxology follows naturally upon every real conversion, for " I say unto you, that likewise joy shall be in heaven over one sinner that repenteth ", Luke xv. 7 ; but there should be the doxology of hearts as well as the doxology of heaven—so Paul's experience leads on to his exultation.

First we have (i) *The Person*—(a) " Now unto the King ". No one is more emphatic than Paul upon the duty of Christians to show loyalty to their earthly sovereign, even though he be a Nero ; yet it is this same teacher who instructs the Thessalonians about " another King, One JESUS ", Acts xvii. 7. When, in any matter, there is a clash of loyalties, it is this Other One that is to be obeyed, for His word is sacrosanct, and His command is superior. This is the Monarch to whom the apostle " now " addresses his worship. (b) " Eternal, immortal, invisible . . . only ". Here are descriptions applied to GOD alone. Eternal— literally, " King of ages " ; that ever was. Immortal—that ever will be. Invisible—for all His reality, that ever remains unseen, except through the mediacy of the Divine Son, John xiv. 9. Only—that abides incomparable ; there is none like Him, He is alone GOD ; yet, not aloof, but alongside, again, in JESUS CHRIST, Matthew i. 23. The overwhelming weight of MS. authority compels us to omit the " wise " in this passage ; though the statement itself is Scriptural, and, indeed, even Pauline—" GOD only wise ", Romans xvi. 27. How we thank GOD—that His love wants what is best for us ; that His power does what is best for us ; and also that His wisdom knows what is best for us—yes, knows what, and knows how. " O loving wisdom of our GOD ", sings Newman. The word is not in this passage, but it is in that other, and is, in truth, embedded in the very eternal reality of the Triune GOD. What a King is He: yet is He, in fact, the King of our lives? Saviour—Friend: but, King? Really?

Well, let us note here (ii) *The Praise*—" be honour and glory, for ever and ever ". His is the glory for every conversion: for Paul's, for Timothy's, for ours. Of course, He does most graciously make use of human instrumentality to that end; only it is not unimportant to point out that our account of the matter is not always correct. When we speak of a person as being the means of the conversion of another, let us not forget that souls are generally brought to GOD, not ropewise, but chainwise. As we are studying this particular Epistle, let us ask, who was the means of Timothy's conversion? We answer, of course, Paul was; for he himself describes his youthful protégé as " my own son in the faith ". Yet, were there not earlier links in the chain? Had Lois no part in it—had Eunice none? Cheer up, ye godly mothers, ye earnest Sunday School teachers, ye faithful pastors: you feel despondent at the seeming lack of fruit, but you may yet discover that you have proved to be a link in a chain, the last link of which may be some evangelist, but all of you together shall have been the chain to bring to GOD that one over whom you have yearned, and prayed, and wept, and worked. Oh the privilege of being a link—the joy of being a last link—the tragedy of being a missing link: a Christian, but caring nothing about the wooing and winning, of wanderers to the Saviour. But, having said all this, it remains the case that the Only Soul-winner is GOD, the HOLY SPIRIT. He uses us in it; but it is He that does it—wherefore all the " honour and glory " belongs to Him. Truly, as II Thessalonians i. 10 reminds us, " He shall come to be glorified in His saints, and to be admired in all them that believe . . . in that day ": so, why not in these days also? And not merely for a little while, but " for ever and ever ". For, praise His Name, His salvation is an " everlasting " salvation, as John iii. 16, and a score of passages assert; and therefore shall His " honour and glory " for it be eternal too. Measureless glory and grace! As Dante Gabriel Rossetti has it—

" . . . . though thy soul sail leagues and leagues beyond,
   still, leagues beyond those leagues, there is more sea."

IV

THE PART PRAYER PLAYS

I TIMOTHY i. 18–ii. 8

18 This charge I commit unto thee, son Timothy, according to the prophecies which went before on thee, that thou by them mightest war a good warfare ;

19 Holding faith, and a good conscience ; which some having put away concerning faith have made shipwreck :

20 Of whom is Hymenæus and Alexander ; whom I have delivered unto Satan, that they may learn not to blaspheme.

1 I exhort therefore, that, first of all, supplications, prayers, inter-cessions, *and* giving of thanks, be made for all men ;

2 For kings, and *for* all that are in authority ; that we may lead a quiet and peaceable life in all godliness and honesty.

3 For this *is* good and acceptable in the sight of God our Saviour ;

4 Who will have all men to be saved, and to come unto the know-ledge of the truth.

5 For *there is* one God, and one mediator between God and men, the man Christ Jesus ;

6 Who gave himself a ransom for all, to be testified in due time.

7 Whereunto I am ordained a preacher, and an apostle, (I speak the truth in Christ, *and* lie not ;) a teacher of the Gentiles in faith and verity.

8 I will therefore that men pray every where, lifting up holy hands, without wrath and doubting.

WHAT a persistent practitioner of prayer Paul was. Over and over again does he touch upon the subject of prayer. He delights to mention the sacrificial use of this ministry in the case of such a man as Epaphras, " always labouring fervently [agonising] for you in prayers ", Colossians iv. 12. He frequently tells us of his own habit of intercession, and occasionally includes in his letters some of the very petitions that he offered on behalf of his friends, and of his children in the faith—to study those actual prayers of his, such as Ephesians i. 15 ff., and iii. 14 ff., is a richly rewarding exercise. And be it noted — especially by those whose particular circumstances make it difficult to pray, who, perchance, have to share a room with another—that Paul was chained to a Roman soldier during much of his prayer-time. Well then, here is this great believer in prayer opening up the matter to this young man as he takes the helm of his diocese, and of his life's work : Paul would have Timothy grasp how great is the part that prayer can play in it all

Of course, there are some who will say that prayer can take no real part in affairs at all : it may be a comfort to the one who prays, it may even have a beneficent influence on his character, but it can have no outside, no objective, effect on the circumstance, or the person, for whom he prays. And this, they would say, for a very simple, and conclusive reason—that the universe is governed by laws, and no prayer can alter them. Our answer is that of course the universe is ruled by laws, and it is by a combination of laws that things happen—but, but, but : prayer itself is one of the laws ! The history of such an institution as Dr. Müller's Orphanage is an imperishable text-book, on that theme ; and so is the story of the China Inland Mission ; and so is the testimony of a myriad Christians who have, in personal experience, proved the truth of the law, and force, of intercession when the proper conditions are observed. The old prayer-warrior who writes these verses knows what he is talking about —he is not just using pious phrases, he is not merely quoting what he has read in books, he is speaking out of his heart, because out of his experience. He knows—let who will deny it—that things do happen in answer to prayer, that prayer has a part, an enormous part, to play in life. For instance—

In Personal Life

On reading the passage i. 18–20, we may be inclined to ask, what has prayer to do with the verses ? It is not mentioned, and does not apparently come into the matter at all. Ah, but look at ii. 1—and study the force of that " therefore ". Because of what he has said about the people he has mentioned, he proceeds at once to urge the necessity for prayer. You notice that three persons are here named ; and first (i) *The One Person who Succeeded.* We see concerning him (*a*) The position—as indicated in those words " this charge ". It is not clear what is referred to ; but my own view is that it is the responsibility laid upon young Timothy to " war a good warfare ", end of verse 18. Some would refer it back to verses 3 and 5, where see my note ; but personally I think it is as I have just said. Note (*b*) the preparation—" according to the prophecies which went before on thee ". Dr. Marvin Vincent renders, " in accordance with prophetic intimations which I formerly received concerning thee ". After all, a gift of prophecy was abroad in the Early Church, and ranked among the foremost of the special spiritual endowments enumerated by Paul, Romans xii. 6; I Corinthians xii. 10. Maybe so ; or maybe as I have written later, on iv. 14. (c) The perseverance—a pressing on in this " warfare " : a word in the Greek which refers not only to the actual fighting, but to all the aspects of a soldier's service. And, by the way, it is not "a", but " the " : the A.V. has the same unfortunate rendering in II Timothy iv. 7, " I have fought a good fight "—which, on the face of it, sounds a bit boastful, until we translate correctly, " the ". Two things will help " son Timothy " in this spiritual soldiering—a taking firm hold of " faith ", an unshakeable trust in his Commanding Officer; and of " a good conscience ", a seeing that he has no consciousness of having played fast and loose with King's Regulations. So (d) The prayers—of Timothy, and for Timothy, will be essential that, in this personal matter of his life, he may make a real success of it. How we prayed for our soldiers personally who went to the World Wars, that they might be kept safe, and that they might do valiantly. How, too, we should pray for those who are enlisted for the World War Army of JESUS CHRIST.

What shall be said of (ii) *The Two Persons who Failed ?* Hymenæus and Alexander, (a) Where they failed—it seems that, in some way, they trifled with their conscience ; and so, as inevitably follows, they shipwrecked their faith, even to the extent that they blasphemed the Holy Name. Let us all take warning, that we treat the dictates of conscience with uttermost care, lest we sear it, and stultify it, and eventually silence it. It is a very delicate instrument—not itself the voice of GOD, but one of His chief means of guiding His children ; it is, as Milton puts it, " the umpire of the soul ", giving the " yea " or " nay " to this or that. And, that this inner voice shall give right decisions, it needs to be assiduously trained and educated by constant assimilating of the Word. (b) What they suffered—" whom I have delivered unto Satan ". It is evident that special gifts were vouchsafed in the Early Days, for promoting and preserving the purity of the church. In the first instance in this passage the gift was prophetic, and now it is punitive. As Dr. Plummer says, " the one existed for the edification, the other for the puri- fication, of the members of the Christian community ". Well now, this delivering unto Satan was a very real tragedy—" the destruc- tion of the flesh, that the spirit may be saved ", as the fate of the incestuous person, in I Corinthians v. 5, is described. You have something of the same sort in the case of Ananias and Sapphira, Acts v., and of Elymas, Acts xiv. Indeed, do not forget that Paul, the erstwhile persecutor, speaks of his physical disability as "the messenger of Satan", II Corinthians xii. 7. I don't understand it ; but there it is. Concerning these two sad failures, I want to ask (c) Why they fell—shall we find the secret in prayerlessness ? Perhaps their fellow-Christians, when they first realised how things were going, tackled the matter in the wrong way—perhaps they argued with them, perhaps they just shrugged their shoulders, perhaps they forbore to pray with them, or even for them. That is, I suppose, all conjecture : or, is it ? I enquire again, Does not the "therefore" of ii. 1 by implication, give us the clue ? Oh, how much opposition might be overcome, how much backsliding might be nipped in the bud, how much Christian progress might be furthered, how much earnest service might be prospered—if only we would pray, and keep on praying, for the persons concerned. We sometimes find people saying, "I'm afraid I can't do anything. I can only pray." Only ? Why, you could never do anything better for people than to pray for them—for the Timothys, in their personal problems and opportunities, that they may make good ; for the Hymenæuses and Alexanders, in their personal temptations to backslide from grace. How great a part prayer can play in this ; as also—

In National Life

There is no doubt that, by the mighty ministry of intercession, we can all of us help to strengthen and to sweeten, the life of the nation, and that, as in this verse, ii. 2, in two directions (i) *That our Leaders may be led aright*—"prayers . . . for kings, and for all that are in authority ". How good a thing it is that Parliament is, each day of its Sittings, opened by prayers, taken by the Chaplain to the Speaker, and that, in an increasing number of cases, City Corporations, and Borough Councils, begin their delibera-tions in the same way. I happen to have had the testimony of the Mayor of one town that, on more than one occasion, the prayer at the beginning has made all the difference to the atmos-phere when tricky and touchy matters have been on the agenda. This is the leaders of the national life praying for themselves ; but our passage lays upon us the responsibility of our praying for them. They have great burdens to bear, they have big problems to solve, they have (many of them) fine ideals to fulfil

—and we can, if we will, help them enormously by our regular and earnest intercession. Most of our local Councils meet in full session on a particular day in the month—the last Monday in each month is the date of the one I know—why not include your own Council on their meeting day in your private prayers ? And Parliament, too—a widespread use of prayer, real and regular, throughout the whole Christian community would accomplish much. And our King—how we thank GOD for the godly testimony of our gracious King and Queen. It is our plain duty to surround and uphold them by our fervent prayers.

All such petitions will further the second desire expressed in our verse, (ii) *That our Life may be lived aright*—" that we may lead a quiet and peaceable life in all godliness and honesty ". Paul is speaking here not of individual, but of national well-being. Note that " quiet " is tranquillity from without—there is no disturbance from outward circumstances ; " peaceable " is tranquillity from within—a nation's heart at rest. This is to be enjoyed, and demonstrated, " in all godliness and honesty " —the first word of which is self-explanatory ; but the second is an unfortunate rendering, inasmuch as the modern significance of honesty is not in the Greek word. The idea is more that of becoming deportment, decency, decorum. E. F. Scott, in the Moffatt Commentary, gives it as " gravity "—which, he says, is " the visible expression of the religious frame of mind ". Here it is, then : a right behaviour, and a right demeanour, which betoken a nation (or, for that matter, an individual) that is right in the sight of GOD.

For another step of desire is here (iii) *That our Lesson may be learned aright*—" for this is good and acceptable in the sight of GOD ". Not in great conquests, not in great industries, not in great discoveries, not in great wealth—though I believe that GOD is not disinterested in such advances and achievements of the human spirit ; yet, not in such like, but in great living is His chief delight. This is a lesson that our country needs desperately to learn afresh, for she once knew it, that " righteousness exalteth a nation ", Proverbs xiv. 34. Many voices are bemoaning these days the wave of moral delinquency that seems to be sweeping through the length and breadth of our beloved land—it isn't only the church that is disturbed, but the police, the magistrates, the scholastic profession, as well. Serious minded people, the country through, are reluctantly confessing that all is not well with our land. Where lies the remedy ? Oh, that the Christians of Britain would wake up to the situation, and that the wave of crime might be matched by a great wave of prayer : that we might see again the part prayer plays in national life. We saw it so recently as the last war in the mighty deliverances that GOD wrought for us, in answer to His people's cry ; may we not see it now in a mighty turning back of the nation's heart to GOD. Such a burden of intercession would secure for us all that guidance, that grit, that gumption, and that grace that are so sorely needed in this hour of the nation's perplexity. The answer to the devil's aeroplanes of destruction is the Lord's prayeroplanes of deliverance. Mark, too, the place of prayer—

IN MINISTERIAL LIFE

Our verses 3–8 deal with the business of " a preacher and . . . a teacher ", verse 7 ; and it leads Paul on to say, " I will therefore that men pray . . . ", verse 8. Would it be permissible, at this point, to ask, " Do you pray for your pastor ? " Is he full of faults ? I dare say. Anyhow, I know one who is. But don't lay all the blame on his shoulders if you have yourself omitted to pray for him. If he is a bit of a failure, he will need those prayers ; if he is a success, perhaps he will need them all the more !

Here in this section we have a fairly representative statement concerning Gospel Ministry. (i) *The Message of the Gospel*— " GOD our Saviour . . . will have all men to be saved, and to come to the knowledge of the truth ", verses 3–4. Such is this inspired proclamation of the wide sweep of the Divine purpose, plan, and provision—there is not a person, never has been, nor ever will be, whom GOD does not wish to save. He has done all that can be done to accomplish that end. In the words of the moving parable of Isaiah v. 1–4, " What could have been done more . . . that I have not done . . . ? " Alas, what hinders is the will of man—which is the one thing that GOD will not force, for that would render him more a machine, and less than a man. The only reason for a soul's being lost is, in the Saviour's words, in John v. 40, that " ye will not come to Me, that ye might have life ". In spite of all His pleadings, the stubborn, sinful will of man persists in rejecting His loving overture, and in refusing His wondrous gift. How all too frequently is the tragedy of Matthew xxiii. 37 re-enacted, " How often would I . . . and ye would not ". That settles it ! GOD can do no more ! What a challenge is here for redoubled earnestness in prayer—that the presentation of the Gospel message may meet with wide acceptance by the will of men everywhere.

We find here, next, (ii) *The Method of the Gospel*—" There is one GOD, and one Mediator between GOD and men, the man CHRIST JESUS ; who gave Himself a ransom for all ", verses 5–6. The church has always had to face the subtle propaganda of false teaching, and in Timothy's day it was the growing dissemination of Gnosticism that was the trouble, as we saw in the first chapter of these studies.   Suficient here to recall that the moral distance between GOD and matter, including man, was such as to require a whole gamut of intermediaries, " æons ", as they were called. Paul, therefore, would underline that the necessity was, not many intermediaries, but " one Mediator ".   How grand an answer is this to Job's perplexity, ix. 33, " Neither is there any daysman betwixt us, that might lay his hand upon us both ". The figure is that of the man who stands between two disputants and reconciles the argument.   The fact is that GOD has provided for us a Divine Daysman to stand between us and Himself.   In His twofold nature, He is in a position to " lay His hand upon us both "—a hand touching Deity, because He is GOD, a hand touching Humanity, because He is " the Man CHRIST JESUS " ; and each hand scarred with the cost of our redemption, the seal of the mediation effected between sinful Humanity and holy Deity, the price of our ransom, demanded by GOD's righteousness, and paid by GOD's love—and that " for all ", on behalf of all, whether they take advantage of it or not.   It is, thus, by the way of sacrificial atonement that our salvation is made possible : that is the method that the Gospel proclaims.   Let us pray that, in these days of self-confidence and self-reliance, when men are seeking to save themselves by another method, preaching and believing " another gospel : which is not another ", Galatians i. 6–7, for there is no other but the one—no other method, " none other name . . . whereby we must be saved ", Acts iv. 12 : let us pray, I say, that a mighty movement of the SPIRIT may bring it to pass that a multitude may " come unto the knowledge of the truth ".

This is the point to introduce (iii) *The Ministry of the Gospel* —" To be testified in due time, whereunto I am ordained a preacher, and an apostle . . . a teacher of the Gentiles in faith and verity ", verses 6–7.   GOD has His duly appointed times for things, even for the things of the Gospel : (*a*) " When the fulness of the time was come, GOD sent forth His Son ", Galatians iv. 4—in preparation for the Gospel. (*b*) " In due time CHRIST died for the ungodly ", Romans v. 6—in provision of the Gospel. (*c*) " To be testified in due time ", our verse 6—in proclamation of the

Gospel. I recall that strange word of the ascending Lord, " but wait ", Acts i. 4, " but tarry ", Luke xxiv. 49. These disciples seemed to have everything now that was requisite for their heralding [the word here translated, " preacher "] of the Gospel message—they had now the knowledge, they had the enthusiasm [note the " great joy " of Luke xxiv. 52], they must have been as dogs straining at the leash to be off ! Why, then, the delay ? The answer is clear in the passages : they had not yet the supreme, the quite indispensable gift, the coming to them of the HOLY SPIRIT. But (d) " When the day of Pentecost was fully come ", Acts ii. 1—the particular " day of Pentecost " that GOD had duly appointed in His calendar for the great Event, then the " wait " was over, the messengers were released upon their errand, and they " began to speak . . . as the SPIRIT gave them utterance ". I press again the question that I posed at the opening of this third main section of this chapter : Do we pray enough for our ministers ? Do we, with earnest longing, beseech the throne of grace that they may be men of the HOLY GHOST, and that their ministry may be so evidently touched and blessed of the SPIRIT that souls shall be born again and built anew. Many a church would be revolutionised if its members would take hold of GOD. I have heard of a famous picture presenting the two apostles Peter and John in characteristic attitudes ; and the caption runs, " While Peter preaches, John prays ". More factually, we recall Exodus xvii. 8–13, whose caption might well read, " While Joshua fights, Moses prays ". No wonder there was glorious victory. And what if—while the pastor preaches, the congregation prays ? Well, we have not finished yet with the part prayer plays in the affairs of men : we see it, lastly—

IN ALL LIFE

As we go back for a final glance at the verses of our passage, we are impressed by Paul's conception of the wide scope, and universal office, of this ministry. We note (i) *The different words* " supplications, prayers, intercessions, thanks ", verse 1. Paul does not use words loosely, but, as guided by the SPIRIT, each has its own specific significance. I wonder if we shall be far wrong if we differentiate between those varied expressions, and say that " supplications " is prayer of particular import, " prayers " is prayer of general import, " intercessions " is prayer of wider import, and " thanks " is prayer of grateful import ? Anyhow, our apostle, by this accumulation of ideas, would give Timothy, as he gives us, a great picture of the vast importance, and variegated implications, of prayer, such as should send him, and us, to practise it with renewed confidence in its ever blessed efficacy.

We have also to take cognisance of (ii) *The diverse people*— (a) Those who are prayed for—" all men ", verse I ; " all men ", verse 4. (b) Those who pray—" men . . . everywhere ", verse 8. The fact is that, not merely a few special men, but men in general, wherever they may be, geographically, or even spiritually, are called upon to engage in this vital exercise. There are, if we may put it so, those who are specialists in prayer ; but there are others, not attaining to that rank, who are nevertheless called upon to be general practitioners of prayer. " Men " of all sorts are to take their part. The further fact is that all men are to be prayed for. No one is so far gone in sin, so deep down in iniquity, that he cannot be reached by this miracle force. Even those who will not allow you to speak to them about GOD, cannot prevent you speaking to GOD about them. What mighty conquests have been won this way—Hudson, a young schoolboy, reading tracts in his father's study one Sunday afternoon while his parents were away for the week-end ; his mother constrained, where she was, to pray specially for her boy, who was called that very afternoon, miles away, to the Saviour, and to become the great Hudson Taylor, of the China Inland Mission. Reuben, a dissolute young man who has left home, has one night got out of bed to commit suicide ; his mother, miles away, has that very hour been constrained also to get out of bed, and to pray specially for her erring son, who, instead of suicide, was saved, subsequently to become the famous American evangelist, Dr. R. A. Torrey. What encouragements to prayer are these, and a myriad other stories. Prayer has, indeed its place, a fragrant place, in all life. As the great Bengel says, " Wherever there are men there are to be found those by whom and for whom prayers are made ".

Let us, however, not forget (iii) *The definite conditions*— " Lifting up holy hands, without wrath and doubting ", verse 8. (a) " Holy hands "—it was the Jewish habit in prayer to lift the hands, palms upwards, as if to receive the answer, cf. I Kings viii. 22 ; Psalm cxxxiv. 2. Such would be the attitude of Elijah, on Carmel's crest, when his prayer became so earnest and urgent that there appeared " a little cloud . . . like a man's hand ", I Kings xviii. 44, as if the prophet's importunity had stamped his hand on the sky. Ah, but " holy hands ". I was having tea at a certain house, when the small son came running in from the garden. Before he could sit down to receive the good things on the table, his mother knowing him, said, " Let me look at your hands ". He was sent out of the room to wash them, and came back to lift up clean hands—holy hands. " If I regard iniquity in my heart [or, in my hands] the Lord will not hear me ", Psalm lxvi. 18. (b) " Without wrath "—that is, no quarrel with any. Do you remember the Master's teaching about " first be reconciled to thy brother, and then come . . . ", Matthew v. 24. Never forget that the harbouring of a grudge will rob your prayer of all effectiveness. (c) " Without . . . doubting." James, a great exponent of effectual prayer, is inspired to counsel any who " ask of GOD " that they are to " ask in faith, nothing wavering ". To doubt the power of prayer, while one prays, is to come under the stricture of the Scripture that says, " Let not that man think that he shall receive anything of the Lord ", James i. 7. Such are some of the conditions of answered prayer —no sin ; no quarrel ; no doubt. And it is available, and applicable, to all life : personal, national, ministerial, all.

How deeply impressed Timothy must have been by all this tremendous emphasis. We may be sure that when this young leader exercises his Oversight, he will not be slow to seek to build up the prayer-life of the believers committed to his charge. And, for himself, we may feel certain that as youth takes the Helm, he will first take hold of GOD.

V

THE LADIES!

I TIMOTHY ii. 9-15

9 In like manner also, that women adorn themselves in modest apparel, with shamefacedness and sobriety ; not with broided hair, or gold, or pearls, or costly array ;

10 But (which becometh women professing godliness) with good. works.

11 Let the woman learn in silence with all subjection.

12 But I suffer not a woman to teach, nor to usurp authority over the man, but to be in silence.

13 For Adam was first formed, then Eve.

14 And Adam was not deceived, but the woman being deceived was in the transgression.

15 Notwithstanding she shall be saved in childbearing, if they continue in faith and charity and holiness with sobriety.

WHAT would the church of CHRIST have done without its women ? Some of them (like the men) have been a nuisance, but so many of them have been such a blessing, to their fellows, and to the Cause. To take but one instance. Go to the Assembly at Philippi. There you will find a pair of ladies at cross-purposes, Euodias and Syntyche, Philippians iv. 2, who threaten to disturb the peace of the whole company, so that Paul has to " beseech " them both to make it up, and not to be stupid. Ah, but on the other hand, there you will discover a lovely soul, in the person of Lydia, Acts xvi. 14-15 ; 40. I wonder how much good she did in her own quiet, unostentatious way. Anyhow, it is of extreme importance that this young Bishop of Ephesus shall know how to handle the female side of church life, and he must have been truly grateful for the guidance that his old mentor gives him, in this Epistle, on this often thorny, and always strategic, matter. So the subject opens—" In like manner also . . . women " : he has been dealing with the " men " ; now, likewise, he will tackle the " women "—and, first, he speaks of—

THE WOMAN AND HER CHARM

He takes just two verses, 9 and 10, to discuss this ; and he divides what he has to say into two kinds of charm (i) *The False Charm that Goes on.* By the way, did you imagine that lipstick

was a purely modern abomination ? Far from that, it was
practised centuries ago by the ancient Egyptians, and other
nations. Old Chrysostom, speaking of the times of this Timothy
letter, mentions " painting, colouring the eyes, a mincing walk,
an affected voice, a languishing look " ; and others have spoken
of " the excess of self-adornment which was the special feature
of the Ephesian women around ". Dr. Plummer's comment
is that, for such things, there is no need to go back to the early
centuries, for " in our own age, and our own church we can find
abundant illustration ". And he was writing fifty years ago !

It seems that Paul is thinking especially of women coming to
worship, and rules that they are not to dress up for such occasion
as if they were going to a theatre, a dance, or a banquet ; but,
indeed, his strictures have a much wider application than only
to church-going—a strict avoidance of vulgar display, whether
in " apparel " or person, is something that " becometh " professing Christian women, wherever they are, and whatever the
occasion. (Incidentally, it seems that men were not [? are not]
entirely free from clothes-worship in church, judging from the
churchwarden's aptitude for showing the be-ringed, and fur-
coated, gentleman into the best seat, which James ii. 2–3 depre-
cates.) Christian women, then, are urged to eschew all that is
unworthy, and unbecoming, in the outward fashions of the
world around them—such as gold-braided hair (a then common
practice, as James Neil tells us in his *Everyday Life in the Holy
Land* "), pearls, or costly array. It seems that, even in those
far-off days, ladies would spend on jewellery and clothes much
more than was proper. These severe words of the apostle are
not to be taken as a plea for frumpishness, but as a warning
against immodesty and extravagance. Ladies ! look nice; but
for pity's sake be natural.

No, if these Christian women seek to know how, outwardly, to
" adorn themselves ", let them be guided by the general principles
behind these three words, (*a*) " modest apparel "—which appears
to include something more than just dress, but to stand for
deportment and demeanour as well; " in seemly guise ", is
Gurney's suggested translation. (*b*) " shame-facedness ", a
particularly unfortunate translation—the word is not easy to
render, but R.V. has the old English word, " shamefastness ",
which Fausset elucidates as " made fast by an honourable
shame ", that is, to allow nothing that would embarrass, or
outrage, a proper sense of shame. (*c*) " sobriety "—nothing to
do with strong drink, though a warning about even that would

not be out of place ; the word really means sobermindedness—a well-balanced state of mind. The way some women bedeck themselves, to bedazzle their friends, betokens a quite different mental condition, hiding and disfiguring any real beauty they may possess.

Enough of that ! Let us turn, with relief, to (ii) *The True Charm that comes out.* Says I Peter iii. 3-4, " whose adorning let it not be that outward adorning of plaiting the hair, and of wearing of gold, or of putting on of apparel [so Peter had the same trouble with the ladies !] but let it be the hidden man of the heart . . . even the ornament of a meek and quiet spirit, which is in the sight of GOD of great price ". Such a spirit will manifest itself, as Paul reminds Timothy, in " good works "—a charm so becoming to a woman " professing godliness ". After all, profession is not merely idle words—if it is true, the words must be matched with the works. You will have noticed, perhaps, that " works " are often mentioned in the Pastoral Epistles in order to oppose the loose living, combined with the loose doctrine, of the false teachers.

If we want to see how attractive, how winsome, this charm can be, we have only to turn again to I Peter iii, where, in verse 1, we have, as I venture rather freely to render it, " Likewise, ye wives, be in subjection to your own husbands ; that, if any respond not to your word [about the Saviour], they also may without [your saying] a word be won by the life of the wives ". Not what you say, but how you act ; not what you profess, but whether you possess ; not only that you believe, but that you behave—there lies woman's, or man's, True Charm. And now, with our passage, let us turn to—

THE WOMAN AND HER CHURCH

Verses 11-14 are occupied with this important relationship. Let it be said at once, before we proceed to an examination of the passage, that church membership is one of the vital matters in the life of a Christian. When we are saved, we are not intended for isolation, but for fellowship : we are " born again " one by one, but we then live as one of a family, the family of GOD, the church of CHRIST. The outward and visible sign of our belonging to *the* church is our membership of *a* church, a Christian assembly, of whatever name, denomination, or character, as seems to us as near, all-round, to the New Testament model as we feel. Into the life and activity of that local church, or assembly, we are wise to throw all our weight, support, and service ; and that, both for the help of the work and witness of that Christian company, and also for the welfare of our own spiritual life and experience. If some young person should ask, " Then can't I be a Christian without going to church ? " the answer is, " Yes ; but you can't be a good one ". It is not for nothing that Hebrews x. 25 says, " Not forsaking the assembling of ourselves together ". I have no hesitation in saying that an isolated Christian is an ill-developed Christian.

Having made which preliminary remarks, we return to our study of our chapter, where we have outlined for us in general terms. the principles of a woman believer's attitude in relation to the worship in her church. By way of warning, let me quote to you these sentences of William Kelly's, " In these times . . . men growingly lose sight of the Divine order in their craving after the imaginary rights of humanity. How many now-a-days are in danger, from a misdirected zeal, or benevolent activity, without due reverence [or even reference, G.H.K.] to the written word." We could wish that the leaders of the women's move- ment in the churches would pause awhile to enquire very seriously whether they are justified in overstepping the barriers that GOD seems to have appointed in His Word. Or—am I all wrong ?

Well then, about the Woman and the Worship, see first, (i) *Her place in the public assembly*—for it is that, and not her ministry in the private circle, that the apostle is speaking of (a) what ? " Let the woman learn in silence with all subjection ". The believer, of whichever sex, should always be a learner— as soon as the LORD's invitation has been obeyed, to " Come unto Me ", it is immediately followed by His instruction, to " Learn of Me ", Matthew xi. 28–9. The woman is to be not one whit behindhand in assuming this attitude of discipleship ; the only difference from the man is that she is herself to make no contribu- tion, by argument, statement, or even question. She is simply to place herself in " subjection " to the teacher, while she maintains a studied " silence ". Any remarks she may wish to make are to be reserved for the privacy of the home after church ! On a recent Sunday morning while having lunch at a boarding- house, I overheard four ladies who had been to a neighbouring church, discussing the service, the sermon, and the speaker. As a preacher myself, I was vastly intrigued with the way we were criticised afterwards by the " silent " women of the con- gregation ! Well, that is What—let them be in school, in sub- jection, and in silence. Now (b) What not ? " I suffer not a woman to teach, nor to usurp authority over the man." To teach in the public assembly is man's GOD-given prerogative, and it is not to be usurped by the woman. Mark, again, he is referring solely to ministry in public worship. He says the same thing in I Corinthians xiv. 34–5, " Let your women keep silence in the churches : for it is not permitted unto them to speak . . . if they will learn any thing, let them ask their husbands at home : for it is a shame for women to speak in the church ". I know, of course, that some people suggest that the Gk. translated " speak " means just to " chatter ", and that this is a prohibition of women chattering in church, which many ladies do—I so wish they wouldn't ! But why make a special point of women, in that case ; for the men are as (or, almost as) bad, and could well do with a like exhortation. Why, then, make this one of the special requirements for the women. But, I very much question whether any reputable Greek scholar would allow that " chatter " is the right rendering. The original word is the same one that is usually given as " speak " in our English Version —for instance, " If any man speak . ..." I Peter iv. 11 ; that is, not chatter, but make an address. Thus, a woman is not to " speak ", in public, in the assembly, nor, as here in I Timothy, to " teach "—that is the man's province and privilege. So that is What not ; but (c) Why ? Two reasons are given for this " subjection " of women—(1) " Adam was first formed, then Eve " —you see, she was made for the second place ; the priority of the elder was the natural order—it is not the priority of the superior, be it noted. I see no evidence of the superiority of man ; but only of his priority. (2) " Adam was not deceived, but the woman "—on the face of it, this seems to be contrary to the fact. Was Adam not deceived ? I think the answer must be, Not directly. Satan's temptation was direct to Eve, but only indirectly, through Eve to Adam. The man was the first in creation ; the woman first " in transgression ". So there it is ! So far as the worship of the public assembly is concerned, the direction is—" that men ", verse 8, should lead the prayer in speech ; and " that women ", verse 9, should adorn the doctrine in silence.

Yet, we must not overlook (ii) *Her position in the early story* —how beautiful and useful a place she occupies in the records of the infant church, and in the days of the Old Dispensation. To keep here to the New Testament — we think of the Virgin Mother ; or of Joanna and Susanna, who " ministered unto Him of their substance ", Luke viii. 3 ; or of Mary Magdalene, and her devotion, John xx. 16 ; or of Martha and Mary, His friends, John xi. 5 ; or of Mary, mother of Mark, who lent her house for the prayer-meeting, Acts xii. 12 ; or of Philip's four daughters, who prophesied, of course in private, Acts xxi. 9 ; or of Lydia, whose heart the Lord opened, and whose house she opened to His servants, Acts xvi. 14–15 ; or of Tabitha, the foundress of Dorcas meetings and all sewing-parties, Acts ix. 39–40 ; or of Phœbe, " Servant of the Church ", and succourer of many ", Romans xvi. 1–2. Continuing the story, we remember Monica who, by her earnest prayers, won over her sadly erring son Augustine to the Saviour's service ; or Maria Millis, nurse companion in the Ashley family, who, by her saintly influence, made the famous Earl of Shaftesbury what he was. Ah, but we have started upon an unending task, if we essay to mention but a tiny proportion of the multitude of godly women, who, though shut off from public ministry, have yet found private opportunities of serving the LORD, and His people. Thank GOD for this grand position that is admiringly, gratefully, and ungrudgingly given them, from the first, in the story of the church. So we go on to emphasise still more clearly—

THE WOMAN AND HER CHANCE

We repeat that she has it (i) *In Private Opportunity.* Let us illustrate this by looking at the instance of Acts xviii. 26, " And he began to speak boldly in the synagogue, whom when Aquila and Priscilla had heard, they took him unto them, and expounded unto him the way of GOD more perfectly ". Of course, they might just have criticised him, and left it at that ; but he was so evidently a good man, that it would have been a pity to leave him where he was. He was a perfectly splendid preacher— eloquent ; mighty in the Scriptures (so far as he went) ; fervent in enthusiasm ; diligent in his work ; courageous. We can well believe that, with all these fine gifts, he drew crowds to the synagogue when he was preaching. And yet there were two members of his congregation who were sadly conscious of some- thing amiss—up to a point this man was magnificent ; but his doctrine was at fault, " knowing only the baptism of John " ! We recall the words of the Baptist himself, " I indeed baptise you with water unto repentance. . . . He shall baptise you with the HOLY GHOST, and with fire ", Matthew iii. 11. Ah, it was that latter thing in which the teaching of Apollos was deficient. You see that in the case of " certain disciples " of his who—upon Paul challenging them on that very matter confessed, " We have not so much as heard whether there be any HOLY GHOST ", Acts xix. 1–2. No ; Apollos had taught them many things ; but they had heard nothing of this doctrine from his lips, because he himself had not known it. It seems that Aquila was too sensitive a soul to take the matter up in public ; but, instead, Apollos was invited to the privacy of the home— one of the benefits of which was that Priscilla was able to join in the talk, and to take her share in the exposition of this all-important subject. It is not said that " he ", Aquila, did it, but that " they " did it : the woman had her chance and she took it. Yes, though debarred from the pulpit in worship, she found the way open to her to bear her testimony, and to give her message, in the women's meeting, in the children's class, and, as in Priscilla's case, in the home circle. How many souls are " in the faith ", II Corinthians xiii. 5, just because faithful women have taken their private opportunity of speaking the word for the Master, which has proved the saving message. GOD be thanked for the ladies, and for their particular ministry.

Our passage speaks further of her chance (ii) *In Parental Responsibility*. " She shall be saved in childbearing ", verse 15. It is a difficult sentence ; and there are two main explanations given of it. (*a*) Giving to " saved " its Gospel meaning, she shall find her own salvation by bringing up her children in faith and love and so on ; but does this not savour of salvation by " works " ? Which Ephesians ii. 8–9 says is inadmissible. (*b*) Still allowing to " saved " its full spiritual significance, and preceding " childbearing " with the definite article, which is there in the Greek, she who was " in the transgression ", verse 14, shall, speaking generically, be saved through " *the* childbearing " of the " seed of the woman " spoken of in Genesis iii. 15. This seems a quite reasonable view to take ; but I personally incline to the opinion that something quite different is intended, that (*c*) " Saved " is not used evangelically, but means here, delivered from spiritual uselessness, for verses 11–14 seem to have condemned the poor lady to that fate. She has her chance, however, in the children that she bears, for, while she cares for all their physical and temporal needs, she can, as no one else can, minister to their spiritual welfare. Hers shall be no repining over a barren life, as she watches them " continue in faith and charity and holiness with sobriety ". If she be denied the joys of normal parenthood, she yet may know the privilege of begetting spiritual children, even as this Paul, who speaks of Timothy as " my own son in the faith ", I Timothy i. 2 ; and through her quiet, personal influence, she may wield a power for the kingdom that is beyond measure, and she may enter with such true understanding into that saying of III John 4, which we have already quoted.

All the same, I think the writer of our passage has in mind, primarily, the children of the ordinary sort—for childbearing is, after all, the normal and natural thing for a woman ; so he refers to woman, as such—and, of course, Christian woman, at that. It is, we say again, in her child that she has her chance. Why, think of the great, and gracious home influence in which " Tiny Tim " had been brought up, even long before Paul had led him to CHRIST. Listen : " I call to remembrance the unfeigned faith that is thee, which dwelt first in thy grandmother Lois, and thy mother Eunice ; and I am persuaded that in thee also ", II Timothy i. 5. Yes, ladies, you have your chance. Indeed, I am not so sure that the public preaching, which is denied you, is a greater, and more powerful ministry than this of the home, which is open to you.

And you, young Timothy, upon whom is thrust so responsible a post as the Oversight of the Ephesian churches, and who will have many believing women in the various assemblies, see that you handle them wisely and well, teaching them these things about their charm, their church, and their chance. And you who owe so much to a woman's touch upon your own spiritual life, make it your care to see that their ministry to others is as happy, and as fruitful, as in your own case.

VI

THEMSELVES FIRST TRAINING FOR THE SKIES

I TIMOTHY iii. 1–16

1 This *is* a true saying, If a man desire the office of a bishop, he desireth a good work.

2 A bishop then must be blameless, the husband of one wife, vigilant, sober, of good behaviour, given to hospitality, apt to teach ;

3 Not given to wine, no striker, not greedy of filthy lucre ; but patient, not a brawler, not covetous ;

4 One that ruleth well his own house, having his children in subjection with all gravity ;

5 (For if a man know not how to rule his own house, how shall he take care of the church of God ?)

6 Not a novice, lest being lifted up with pride he fall into the condemnation of the devil.

7 Moreover he must have a good report of them which are without ; lest he fall into reproach and the snare of the devil.

8 Likewise *must* the deacons *be* grave, not double-tongued, not given to much wine, not greedy of filthy lucre.

9 Holding the mystery of the faith in a pure conscience.

10 And let these also first be proved ; then let them use the office of a deacon, being *found* blameless.

11 Even so *must their* wives *be* grave, not slanderers, sober, faithful in all things.

12 Let the deacons be the husbands of one wife, ruling their children and their own houses well.

13 For they that have used the office of a deacon well purchase to themselves a good degree, and great boldness in the faith which is in Christ Jesus.

14 These things write I unto thee, hoping to come unto thee shortly :

15 But if I tarry long, that thou mayest know how thou oughtest to behave thyself in the house of God, which is the church of the living God, the pillar and ground of the truth.

16 And without controversy great is the mystery of godliness : God was manifest in the flesh, justified in the Spirit, seen of angels, preached unto the Gentiles, believed on in the world, received up into glory.

You will probably recall Bishop Armstrong's beautiful Ordination hymn, " O Thou who makest souls to shine ", in which the lines occur—

> " Themselves first training for the skies,
> They best will raise their people there."

That is how it is in our passage, which deals with the leaders of the churches, and teaches that if those leaders would lead others aright, they must themselves be led aright. Look, then at—

THE MAJOR OFFICE

" *The office of a bishop* " (1) is not to be confused with the modern bishopric. Timothy did not wear gaiters, nor a shovel hat. Yet, it was a position of very real responsibility, and ofttimes of much danger. That was what gave it its particular character as " a good work ", and made it something to be " desired ". By the way, the word rendered thus has really a considerably stronger connotation : it indicates, not merely a passive waiting for, but an active reaching for—an eager coveting. In the early church, it was not the easy posts, the placid positions, that were sought after, but the hard, and even perilous jobs. It is a striking example of the enthusiasm of those first believers that they, many of them, actually coveted martyrdom ; while too many of us curl up at the first sight of opposition. Well now, in the light of all its heavy responsibilities, what are the special qualifications for such an office ? Remember that Paul is very particularly stressing these things for Timothy's sake, as he takes up the office ; and remember, too, that much of what he says is applicable also to any kind of Christian life and service. Examine it, therefore, part by part.

" *Blameless* "—without reproach ; giving no just handle to anyone to point the finger of scorn, or of rebuke. Of course, there will always be those inimical, or irresponsible persons who will abuse the best of men. Even such fine rulers of the flock as Ignatius, Polycarp, Cyprian, and Chrysostom suffered such criticism. But the point to determine is whether it is just criticism, or not. Do you not think that that should be our first reaction to any criticism of ourselves—not to fly into a rage, not to threaten to leave the church, not to answer back ; but, first, is what they accuse us of true ? If so, let us seek GOD'S grace to amend it ; if not, then we can assuredly afford to ignore it. That's it—whether for bishops, or for ourselves : see that there is no reasonable cause to reproach us, for any sayings, or doings of ours. The world is only too ready to catch us out, if it can : let us, therefore, be on our guard.

" *The husband of one wife* "—It is extremely difficult to say what the apostle means by this. Where the learned doctors disagree, it ill behoves a tyro to presume to decide. I think,

however, that we may simplify the matter down to two alternatives : either (*a*) that he must not have more than one wife at a
time ; or (*b*) that, if his wife die, he must not marry another.   The
first seems very unlikely, since, even among the Greeks and
Romans, polygamy was unknown ; and such an occurrence in
the Christian church would have scandalised the heathen world
itself.   Such a prohibition would surely be most unnecessary—
bishop, or no bishop.   With the greatest deference, therefore,
I offer the suggestion that it is the second of our alternatives
that Paul is commending : that, in the marriage union, the wife
and husband become so intimately " one flesh ", that another
cannot take the dead one's place.   I Corinthians vii. 8–9 ;   39–40
seem to suggest possible exceptions to the rule ; or, shall we say
that the injunction (" must ", verse 2) is for bishops, while the
laity are allowed a certain latitude " in the LORD ".   No reason
seems to be given for such a distinction, if it be there ; but
perhaps, if we knew more of the circumstances of that age, and
of that Ephesus, the matter would be apparent.   Frankly, I
don't know ; doubtless other people do know—personally, I
haven't yet come across them.   Of one thing we may be quite
sure : that neither Paul, nor the HOLY SPIRIT who inspired him,
would teach anything that, in any way, would weaken, or loosen,
the sanctity of the marriage vow.   This sacred matter is one of
the big things to be guarded by the Office of the Oversight—
and the bishop himself must be the first to observe, and exemplify,
it.   Let that suffice for this exordium.

" *Vigilant* "—Here, at least, we are on sure ground.   Says
I Peter v. 8, " Be vigilant, because your adversary the devil, as
a roaring lion, walketh about " ; but not only as the lion, for
" we are not ignorant of his devices . . . for Satan himself is
transformed into an angel of light ", II Corinthians ii. 11 ; xi. 14.
In how many, sometimes startling, sometimes subtle, ways does
he seek to undermine, or overthrow, the unwary.   Perhaps his
chief onset is still to throw doubt upon the Word of God, as in
the first days, " Yea, hath GOD said . . . ? " Genesis iii. 1, for he
fears it so, as we see in our LORD's use of Deuteronomy in the
Temptation, Matthew iv. 4, 7, 10.   One of Shakespeare's characters says that " The devil can quote Scripture to his purpose " ;
but he generally quotes it wrong, as in Matthew iv. 6.   That is
why it is so important, when the sowers of false doctrine quote
the Bible to support their claims, to be on the alert against their
" wresting the Scriptures ", II Peter iii. 16, and tearing texts
from their contexts.   One of the gravest responsibilities laid upon

the bishop is that he be vigilant against all unscriptural teaching, and all attacks—open or secret—of the evil one. Indeed, all believers are thus to be wary.

" *Sober* "—this is not to be construed as an instruction to bishops that they are not to get drunk, even though the particular bishop here addressed is advised to take " a little wine " medicinally (I Timothy v. 23). A " little " can so easily grow to a lot, if we are unwatchful. And there have been drunken bishops ! I seem to remember, from my schooldays, that an old Latin author said, " The corruption of the best is the worst ". But no, this word has nothing to do with that failing. A reference to that comes in the next verse. We shall the more readily grasp the significance of this word if we render it—" sober-minded ". It pictures, as Canon Liddon said, " a man of calm, unimpassioned mind "—" collected, unexcitable, well composed ", as another writes. Such a man, such a bishop, will not speak rashly, will be a person of sound judgment, will be master of himself, and of his situation. It is easy to be seen how commendable a quality this is in one who is called to exercise any sort of leadership among men.

" *Of good behaviour* "—a bishop must not only talk well, but walk well. Isn't that incumbent upon us all ? One is reminded of the resolution of David, in Psalm ci. 2, " I will behave myself ". As the old negro preacher said, " Dere be two sides to de Gospel : dere's de beliebing side, and dere's de behabing side "—quaintly put, but exactly true. As the Epistle of James teaches us, ours is to be a belief that behaves. A bishop, then, is to practise what he preaches ; there is to be no manner of inconsistency between what he says, and what he does, and what he is. So often godly conduct has proved efficacious when earnest exhortation has failed. When a maid was asked, " Under whose preaching were you converted ? " she replied, " It wasn't nobody's preaching, it was mother's practising ". It has so frequently been that way. Mind you, we do not disparage the preaching : no one can do that who has I Corinthians i. 21 in mind. Paul will press that part of a bishop's duty later ; but, for the moment, he stresses the ministry of the life, as backing up the ministry of the lip. A young doctor met an old schoolfellow that he had not seen for years. The latter said, " Let me see, didn't you have a brother at school ? What are you both doing nowadays ? " To which the doctor replied, on behalf of his parson brother, and himself, " Yes, there were the two of us : and now my brother preaches, and I practise ". Well, what the true servant of GOD displays is a combination and co-operation of both.

" *Given to hospitality* "—there is a surprising emphasis in the New Testament on the duty of this ministry among Christians. There is no doubt that, for those who are in a position to exercise it, this is a most fruitful form of Christian service ; but we must remember that the injunction carried a peculiarly important onus in the days of the Early Church. Such was the deep cleavage between the Christian and the heathen manner of life that a travelling believer could not possibly stay under the roof of a pagan's dwelling ; and it was therefore essential that disciples of the Master should go out of their way to care for one another in this fashion whenever the need should arise. So Lydia, of Philippi, opened her house to Paul and Silas, as soon as she opened her heart to the Lord, Acts xvi. 15, 40. A modern bishop's house is a veritable hive of hospitality !

" *Apt to teach* "—instruction, on the positive side ; refutation, on the negative side. Such are the two aspects of the teaching ministry : each of them so essential, in our time, as in Timothy's day. Much false teaching is abroad ; and, in the main, the apostle's method of counteracting it is by true teaching. In the Ephesian church there was a variety of spiritual gifts, for the well-being of the body of believers—some few had the special gift of apostleship, some that of prophesying, some that of evangelism, some that of shepherding the converts and teaching them in the faith, Ephesians iv. 11-12. So that instead of remaining baby-Christians, tossed about with any prevailing wind of cunning heretical teaching, they may become full-stature Christians, able to stand firm, and to help to anchor others. Timothy will be called upon for a good deal of this kind of work —a work, indeed, so proper to the Oversight.

" *Not given to wine* "—the word implies not sitting over wine, not behaving ill at wine, not becoming quarrelsome over it. How oft this might ensue from a lingering over the cups. A bishop must be doubly careful to avoid any such habit : he is the leader, and if he is slack about this, his flock will quickly follow. For their sakes, as well as for his own, he must forego any inclination to this fault. You see, any Christian leader has, perforce, to set for himself a very high standard in all things.

" *No striker* "—don't mistake this for an order that he is not to " down tools ". The idea is that he is not to be a violent man, not combative nor pugnacious—" with hand or tongue ", adds Fausset. Some people's tongue is a deadly weapon—just how devastating it can be is seen in James iii. 5-8—a fire, a beast, a poison. How we need, all of us, constantly to use the Psalmist's prayer, " Keep the door of my lips " Psalm cxli. 3. Our harmful speech is generally hasty and unpremeditated, it just slips out —but then the hurtful thing is done. Oh, to be able to recall it. We shall not be amongst those wicked people who say, " Our lips are our own : who is lord over us ? ", Psalm xii. 4—GOD is Lord over us, and our lips are not our own. We are accountable to Him for our words, as for our deeds and thoughts. So our bishop is not to be characterised by violent speech, violent temper, nor violent action. The gentle Timothy is not likely to be a " striker " —but the HOLY SPIRIT has caused it to be put in writing for the benefit of all leaders in spiritual things. It is all too possible for those who are ahead to become aggressively impatient with those who cannot think so quickly, or act so exactly, as their superiors think they should.

" *Not greedy of filthy lucre* "—money is not evil in itself ; many moneyed men have been, and are, godly men : Abraham in the Old Testament, Joseph of Arimathæa in the New, and many such since. It becomes evil only when it is ill-gotten, or ill-spent ; then is it " filthy " lucre. Are we surprised that it is needful to warn against this, and all these wrong things ? We must remember that these early Christians had only just come out of heathendom, where such evils were rife. A specifically Christian conscience was only beginning to be created, and things which in their old unconverted days were quite natural, were scarcely yet regarded with the significance that they later acquired. Paul will have something to say presently about " the love of money ", I Timothy vi. 10. Just now he is concerned to warn his young friend, and all church leaders, against the all-too-common sin of avarice. Gold may be a god-send ; but, beware, it may be a devil-bait. Remember Judas, who " had the bag ", and helped himself. John xii. 6.

" *Patient* "—" forbearing " is the better rendering : a quality of mind and heart that makes allowances for slownesses, awkward-nesses, even rudenesses, of others. Such an attitude of gentleness may have much to put up with, but it will win in the end—and it will have the incomparable advantage of not only winning the point, but also winning the man ; whereas positional pomposity, while gaining the argument, may strangle the allegiance. " Let patience have her perfect work ", James i. 4, is the inspired rule. It would seem that this is a recommendation applicable to bishops of all ages : an overbearing personality defeats its own ends.

" *Not a brawler* "—this appears to follow naturally upon the previous quality, for the point here is that he is to be a " peaceable " person : not, mark you, peace at any price, but peace at every possibility. " First pure, then peaceable ", James iii. 17, is the scriptural order. While the bishop, like the rest of us, is to " earnestly contend for the faith once delivered . . .", Jude 3, he is not to be a contentious man. He must be on his guard against stirring up strife, by any word or action. His invariable counsel to his flock will be that they " be at peace among yourselves ".

" *Not covetous* "—the last of the Ten Words, " Thou shalt not covet . . .", Exodus xx. 17, is not the least important of them ; for it is probably true to say that more evil results follow from covetousness than from almost any other sin. Although the actual word Paul uses here means money-loving, the application may assuredly be made to coveting in any form—to covet any possession, or any position, not our own, is to lay ourselves open to all kinds of virulent temptation, in order to secure the thing we so strongly desire. Oh, to learn, with this same apostle, in Philippians iv. 11, " I have learned, in whatsoever state I am, therewith to be content ".

" *One that ruleth well his own house* "—a man who is called to the Oversight is, in a very real sense, under GOD, the head of the house : he must have learned his trade by success in headship on a lower plane. If he is not able to govern the house of his own, he can scarcely be likely to govern the Household of GOD. It is not every family, not even every episcopal family, that is ordered by the twin-rule of devotion and discipline ; but it should be so, and success in the lesser sphere is splendid training for the wider responsibility. And how important is all this for the children's own sake. For good, or for ill, the deepest influence in a child's life is normally the home—and nothing is more likely to instil proper ideas of life, and proper principles of behaviour, and proper ideals of ambition, than what is taught and learnt there by way of precept and practice. What a bishop does for his own children is calculated to help him greatly in dealing with his spiritual children in his enlarged oversight.

" *Not a novice* "—no one is to be appointed to the office of Overseer who is but yet a beginner, a " neophyte ", a recent convert ; the position calls for a man of experience, of the truth he teaches, of the life he expounds, of the world he serves, of the warfare he wages, of the people he leads. There have been, and are, exceptions where quite young men have entered successfully into posts of leadership. Bishop Timothy himself was a comparative youth when he took the helm of the " diocese " of Ephesus. Still, speaking in general, people, with all their admiration and esteem for young men's qualities and gifts, do look for that touch which experience gives in their spiritual leaders. As for the " novice " himself, eminence is all too liable to engender within him the sin of pride—the very thing for which, it seems, the devil fell into condemnation.

" *A good report* "—it is interesting that the testimonial is to be won from " them which are without " : not from the believers, but from the worldlings. The world is often a pretty shrewd judge of character, and all too ready an observer of insincerity and inconsistency. It will be part of a bishop's ambition, not to win applause, but to earn approval from those who are outside his faith : indeed, if his character and conduct be of a truly godly sort it will often prove a strong lever for bringing those others within the fold. Looking back upon all that has been written here, we remark again how high a level of life is demanded of those who have been called to leadership in the ways and things of GOD. It is time that we now gave our attention to—

THE MINOR OFFICE

" *The office of a deacon* ", verse 13. This was appointed, as we learn from Acts vi. 2–3, to deal with the material side, the " business " affairs, of the church life. Even so, very high spiritual quality was demanded of its members—indeed, that they be men " full of the HOLY GHOST ", as well as of " wisdom ", which in this context I suppose means business acumen. Let it be remembered that this body of the church's business men included such flaming evangelists as Stephen and Philip. The church has ever since been often indebted to its laymen for great spiritual aid and adventure. Still, the more material aspects are, naturally, their particular department ; though, be it added, the spiritual leaders are not always so lacking in financial and business ability as they are commonly supposed to be ! As a matter of fact, it has been doubted whether the " deacon " here is the lineal descendant of those in Acts vi., or whether he is of a quite different order. There is of course, understandably enough, some measure of development, owing amongst other things to the widespread growth of the church, and consequently, of the need ; but as to the virtual correspondence of the two bodies, I am myself convinced by " the common opinion of the Early Church from Irenæus onwards that they were identical " (Gurney). Now, what are the stated qualifications for the members of this junior office ? In large degree, they are the same as those for the senior service, and to that extent do not call for any reiteration of treatment; but let us pick out the one or two things that are mentioned as belonging peculiarly to the deacon.

" *Grave* "—I suppose that means seriously minded, an absence of flippancy. There is real danger in the rather jocose use of spiritual things, such as Bible stories, and Christian matters, and sometimes the layman is particularly guilty. Make no mistake about it, the Christian life is meant to be a very happy thing, and we are not intended to dwell in a miserable hiatus of dull negativism; but, for all that, it is a sacred and solemn thing, and is not to be conceived of with unbecoming levity. A proper gravity is no foe to a happy spirit; but it *is* opposed to a shallow jocularity—which matches ill with the responsibilities of the deacon's office.

" *Not double-tongued* "—" making different representations to different people about the same thing ", says Dr. Vincent; saying one thing, meaning another; accommodating our opinion to our company. That kind of thing, which is reprehensible in any of us, is particularly detrimental in the work of a deacon, whose duties call for straight dealing, and decided speech. Let us all be careful that people shall come to know that if we say a thing we mean it, if we promise a thing we keep it, if we undertake a thing we carry it through—that, as it used to be said, " An Englishman's word is his bond ", so now it may be understood that a Christian's word is his bond. So then, beware the snare of saying what we believe will be agreeable and popular even though it be slightly away from the truth.

" *A pure conscience* "—it is not enough that a deacon or any other believer hold the mystery of the faith in an orthodox fashion, though that is of deep importance; but he must be " proved ", or tested, to see that his life is blameless, that his conscience is clear as before GOD and as touching his fellows. Handling monetary things as he does, the deacon must be meticulously careful that he deviate not the slightest fraction from the straight and upright. Many a Christian business man has found himself in a very serious situation, not from any criminal intention, but simply from careless inattention to doubtful detail. Just now we were cautioned against levity, this time it is against laxity, and in pursuance of loyalty to the GOD whom we serve. In this regard, as in all others, let us follow Paul in his confession before Felix, " Herein do I exercise myself, to have always a conscience void of offence toward GOD, and toward men " Acts xxiv. 16.

" *Even so . . . their wives* "—As Vincent says, " A deacon whose wife is wanting in the qualities required in him, is not to be chosen. She would sustain an active relation to his office, and by her ministries would increase his efficiency, and by frivolity, slander, or intemperance, would bring him and his office into disrepute ". How true, in both regards, has this proved to be the case. This office-bearer's wife must strive to be " faithful in all things "—in her home duties, in her personal character, in her husband's support. Let us leave it at that—staying only to underline the fact of what joy it is when husband and wife are thus in complete and happy accord in the service of the LORD. Truly, in that case, " two are better than one "—and if they have a child also in the work, then the " threefold cord is not quickly broken ", Ecclesiastes iv. 9, 12.

" *A good degree* "—this is, of course, not a University degree ; though school and university combine, in this chapter, in a curiosity : " good work " (verse 1), " good behaviour " (verse 2), " a good report " (verse 7), and now " a good degree " (verse 13). The word really means " a good standing ", as the Revised Version renders it. We might almost say, " a step up ". You may recall that Psalms cxx–cxxxiv are entitled, " Songs of Degrees ", and it is suggested that they were appointed to be sung as the pilgrims went up the steps to the Temple. Remember, too, how, in II Kings xx. 11, the " shadow " of the sundial of Ahaz returned backward ten " degrees ", which, again, were probably the Temple steps. Yes, I think we may be certain that this faithful deacon will have a good step up, will have earned promotion in the service of his LORD. Alas, it has sometimes happened that, because of unfaithfulness, servants of GOD have had to step down from the high prominence that once they held in Christian work. Let us grasp the solemn fact that, however high we may reach in holiness and service, we shall never get beyond the need for earnest watchfulness. And now our chapter closes with a few words going back to the proper discharge of Timothy's major office, and then concludes with a brief reference to—

THE MESSIANIC OFFICE

How utterly majestic is this statement, how breath-taking the phrases, spite of their simplicity. They have the rhythm of a hymn, and the form of a creed—an epitome of doctrine concerning our Lord JESUS CHRIST. Ponder the great truths, clause by clause. Actually, the divine Name does not appear in any of the most ancient MSS., which all begin the passage with " Who ", or " He Who " ; but if the word is not there, the fact of His Deity is implicit throughout.

" *Manifest in the flesh* "—His eternal existence is understood. He did not begin at birth, any more than He ended at death ; but Bethlehem was the point at which He showed Himself to man. In order to fulfil the blessed mission on which He was to embark, " a body hast Thou prepared Me ", Hebrews x. 5 ; and in that human body He made His appearance amongst us on earth. It was as I John i. 2 describes it, " The life was manifested, and we have seen it . . . that eternal life, which was with the Father, and was manifested unto us ". That Form, whose feet trod the ways of Galilee and the waters of Gennesaret, was the very same Form of the Fourth ", Daniel iii. 25, that walked in the fire to rescue the three, and is come down now to " deliver " from the fire again. Here, then, in such simple terms is stated the amazing fact of the Incarnation of the Son of GOD.

" *Justified in the spirit* "—The chief purpose of His " manifestation " was that He might die, whereat His last words were, " Father, into Thy hands I commend My spirit ", Luke xxiii. 46. At the Cross, He " was delivered [because of] our offences ", and subsequently " was raised again [because of] our justification ", Romans iv. 25. Because He had accomplished the means of our justification, which was what He came to do, GOD justified His action, in offering His spirit even unto death, by signifying His acceptance of the sacrifice by raising Him from the dead. He was " declared to be the Son of GOD with power [the acknowledgement of the efficacy of His saving power] according to the SPIRIT of holiness by the resurrection from the dead ", Romans i. 3.

" *Seen of angels* " — Doubtless, angels had watched His departure to this earth, watched with wonder His human growth from childhood to manhood, watched with bated breath His battle-royal in the wilderness, watched with delight as He went about doing good, watched over Him when His intimates could not watch with Him one hour in the garden, watched, as " the winged squadrons of the sky ", for the signal that never came to rescue Him from infamous arrest, watched with veiled faces throughout the excruciating hours of Golgotha—all this, in all likelihood. But, in this credal sequence, I imagine that the reference is to the arrival of the angelic warders, sent by the Heavenly Governor, to open the prison-door of death, seeing that, having completed His sentence, it was no longer " possible that He should be holden of it "— Acts ii. 24, they were the very first to see " the Living One, that was dead ", Revelation i. 18. Not till afterwards was He seen of men—of Mary and the women ; " of Cephas . . . of the twelve . . . of the five hundred . . . and last of all [as Paul avers] . . . of me also ", I Corinthians xv. 5–8. What joyful tidings would those " angels " take back to their fellows, awaiting news of the success of their mighty errand to the Tomb.

" *Preached unto the Gentiles* "—or, rather, unto the nations ; for this news was not for Jews only, but for all peoples throughout the wide world. The promulgation at Pentecost, Acts ii. 8–11, was followed by the propagation at large. Be it noted that the tidings were not of an extraordinary " it " but of a wonderful " Him "—not a thing, not a movement, not an experience, but a Person. It is " He who . . . was preached "—for it is He who in Himself is the Gospel ; Christianity is CHRIST. This commission to preach Him is laid upon us also, as well as on those earliest disciples ; and to refrain from that duty is criminal selfishness, withholding the water of life from souls dying from thirst ; is plain disloyalty, refusing His orders to " go " and do it ; is evident stupidity, making, as it will, for spiritual ill-health of those who take in only and never give out.

" *Believed on in the world* "—for, " your labour is not in vain in the LORD ", I Corinthians xv. 58 ; and " He that goeth forth and weepeth, bearing precious seed, shall doubtless come again with rejoicing, bringing his sheaves with him ", Psalm cxxvi. 6. This " Word of Life " is precious seed indeed, and while in some there is no response, in others there is full result—all down the age, all through the world, thank GOD, He is believed on. Mark that preposition : it is not believed *about*, acceptance of the historical fact ; neither is it believed *in*, acknowledgment of the spiritual power; but it is believed *on*, abandonment to the personal Saviour. " A great multitude, which no man could number, of all nations, and kindreds, and people, and tongues ", Revelation vii. 9, have come to believe on Him—have you, my reader ? At each point of time, perchance, only a small minority —" few there be ", Matthew vii. 14 ; always but a " little flock ", Matthew xii. 32. Yet in the eventual aggregate such a vast multitude of wondering, worshipping souls.

" *Received up into glory* "—is this not out of proper order : did not His ascension precede the preaching and the believing ? Yes ; but the commission to preach, whose fulfilment and fruit are in those previous phrases, was given before—and immediately before—His being received up. Mark xvi. 15–16 ; 19. Acts i. 8–9. Can you imagine the joy with which He was welcomed back to the Glory ; and can you enter into the joy with which His disciples bade Him farewell, Luke xxiv, 51–2 ? A joy that had its roots in a certain understanding of what His ascension means to Him, and what it means for us who do believe on Him, and who therefore, as Paul is careful to point out to this very Timothy's Ephesians (ii. 5–6), are by His grace, and through our faith, united to Him, identified with Him, in it all.

The proclamation of this Messiah—who came, and who is coming again, I Timothy vi. 14—is the blessed ambition of bishops and deacons, and of us all, ourselves " first training for the skies ".

VII

BAD NEWS AND GOOD ADVICE

I TIMOTHY iv. 1-11

1 Now the Spirit speaketh expressly, that in the latter times some shall depart from the faith, giving heed to seducing spirits, and doctrines of devils ;

2 Speaking lies in hypocrisy ; having their conscience seared with a hot iron ;

3 Forbidding to marry, *and commanding* to abstain from meats, which God hath created to be received with thanskgiving of them which believe and know the truth.

4 For every creature of God *is* good, and nothing to be refused, if it be received with thanksgiving :

5 For it is sanctified by the word of God and prayer.

6 If thou put the brethren in remembrance of these things, thou shalt be a good minister of Jesus Christ, nourished up in the words of faith and of good doctrine, whereunto thou hast attained.

7 But refuse profane and old wives' fables, and exercise thyself *rather* unto godliness.

8 For bodily exercise profiteth little : but godliness is profitable unto all things, having promise of the life that now is, and of that which is to come.

9 This *is* a faithful saying and worthy of all acceptation.

10 For therefore we both labour and suffer reproach because we trust in the living God, who is the Saviour of all men, specially of those that believe.

11 These things command and teach.

THE Bible is a book so true to life—while it delights to record the good, it does not attempt to hide the evil. Abraham's deception, Moses' outburst, Elijah's juniper, Uzziah's end ; it tells the glowing story of Gideon, but does not omit the sad blot on the last page. When the artist came to execute a portrait of Oliver Cromwell, the Protector commanded him to make it a true likeness—" paint me wart and all ". That is how it is with the Bible portraits—wart and all. That is how it is, also, when the Scriptures delineate the conditions of life—they are never afraid to tell the bad news ; but, thank GOD, alongside will be found the good advice that will serve to meet the situation. Thus it is in this passage. Paul is so anxious that the young bishop shall be prepared for the trouble that he will meet, in the form of false teaching, so he offers the inspired advice for him and his flock.

A Caution—to Beware

This is dealt with in verses 1–5. And first in *the Contrast stated*—" Now ", which should be " But ". Great and glorious things have been unfolded at the close of the previous chapter : here it is all so different. It is as if we had been traversing a lovely road, full of fine houses and beautiful gardens, and then turned a corner into a lane of dirty, tumble-down, slum property, abounding in weeds, and rank disfigurement. " But " is to me always, for good or ill, the corner-word of Scripture. Timothy will find much of good cheer and encouragement in his Oversight ; " but "—let him beware—there will be also things that are ugly and evil.

We stay to mark *the Importance assumed*—" the Spirit speaketh expressly ". In all reverence, let us remark that the Holy Spirit does not speak just for the sake of speaking : the matters now to be mentioned are of such high moment that He makes a very especial point of speaking about them. It seems to me that if we have any real belief in the divine inspiration of the Bible, we must hold it all as of great importance—even the seemingly small things. We may take it for granted that it was not for nothing that God caused that detail to be recorded. Why, for example, in John vi. 4, say that " the passover . . . was nigh " —the fact appears to have no relevance to the subject. Is it, do you think, to account for the statement later that " there was much grass in the place "—which would be the case only at Passover time, the rest of the year there being bereft of vegetation. Be sure that everything in the Bible is there for a purpose, since it is the Spirit's work. The purposefulness of the present passage is particularly pressed by the use of the word that He speaketh " expressly ".

That being so, let us next examine *the Time expressed*—" in the latter times ". It seems to mean, times future to the time of writing. The matter envisaged by the apostle, though possibly in bud as he writes, will not be in bloom until later. This is the more likely by reason of the fact that there is no definite article in the Greek ; and " in latter times " would be a quite proper rendering, with the significance of " later on ". It is very different with the phrase of II Timothy iii. 1—" in the last days ", where the reference is to the period at the close of the present age, immediately prior to the Paronsia, the Return of our Lord JESUS. This latter is a time that is constantly in the apostle's mind— in his last Epistle as well as in his first ; but, in our present study, he is thinking of conditions in the nearer future. Oh, to be ready for either ; and to be able to rest, with the Psalmist, in the knowledge that " My times are in Thy hands ", Psalm xxxi. 15 —our past redeemed ; our present surrounded ; our prospect assured.

And now for *the Trouble prophesied*—" some shall depart from the faith ". From the body of truth, from the body of believers. Speaking from the opposite point of view, Paul has a remarkable word in II Corinthians xiii. 5, " Examine yourselves, whether ye be in the faith ". That is a testing enquiry for every Church member : is his allegiance merely nominal, or is it real ? Is his profession of Christianity only an outward thing ? A true Christian is a Christ-in-one : is this fundamental characteristic ours, or is our confession, however beautiful, only outside veneer ? Remember that one time there were those who were thought to be " in the faith ", counted as being among the sheep, but they " departed from the faith ", they deserted the fold—and thereby, according to II Peter ii. 22, proved that they never had been sheep, but were, though in sheep's clothing, all the time dirty dogs and filthy pigs. Many a so-called backslider has, as a matter of fact, never been a genuine Christian. Was it thus with the professors of our passage ? Anyhow—

It is time we considered *the Source indicated*—" giving heed to seducing spirits, and doctrines of devils ". We must not suppose that Satan himself honours us with his personal atten- tions as he did with our Lord in the wilderness ; but he has his armies of evil spirits who are sent forth to compass the downfall of unwary believers with their devilish doctrines. These impious beings are expert in the unholy art of " seducing ", choosing their victim and their moment with cunning precision. They come to a man at a time of intellectual doubt, or of devastating sorrow, or of spiritual failure, or even of bodily weakness—and they insinuate the seed of what is false, which becomes in course of time the very ruin of a soul, the catastrophe of a life, as in the instance of these unfortunate persons of whom Timothy is here warned. Let none of us suppose that we are to be immune from such attacks or free from such dire results. It behoves us all to exercise eternal vigilance.

There seems to follow now *the Agents described*—" speaking

lies in hyprocisy; having their conscience seared with a hot iron ". This appears to refer to the human instruments of the wicked spirits; for the evil spirit is ever aping the HOLY SPIRIT —in this, as in so many other ways, that he employs human agency to further his fell designs. It is a startling thought that even the keenest Christians, off their guard, can become the actual tools of the devil—" Get thee behind Me, Satan ", Matthew xvi. 23, was spoken to Peter, because he had been temporarily seduced into doing the Evil One's work. Poor see-saw Peter— so high one moment; so low the next as to allow himself to be the foul fiend's catspaw. Writer and reader—beware ! See then how these wretched agents will go to work. Their conscience, once so sensitive, is now " seared ", as flesh would be by the application of a " hot iron ", rendering it almost dead. Time was when they would shrink in horror from the uttering of a " lie ", but now that conscience is silenced, they can do it without blushing, with the tongue of " hypocrisy " in their cheek. How, if unchecked, evil grows in a man, on a man.

We come now to *the Question raised*—" forbidding to marry, and commanding to abstain from meats ". This sounds like the early beginnings, as we saw in an earlier Study, of the heresy of the Gnosticism that so greatly troubled the church in the second century, and which Paul had to deal with so strongly in Colossians—a teaching whose prohibitive tenets were based on what they held to be the inherent evil of matter, as such. This body seems to have owed much to the sect of the Essenes, an ascetic Jewish brotherhood who, to quote Dr. Vincent, " repudiated marriage except as a necessity for preserving the race, and allowed it only under protest and under strict regulations. They also abstained strictly from . . . animal food." This falsity created something like havoc in some of the early churches, not least so in Ephesus, which was within Timothy's spiritual charge. Is it not strange what specious, devil-promulgated doctrines have made mischief among believers all down the age ? From such speciousness we are not exempt to-day—their titles generally ending in " -ism " or " -ist ".

Naturally, we want to know *the Reply given*—" which GOD hath created to be received with thanksgiving of them which believe and know the truth. For every creature of GOD is good, and nothing to be refused, if it be received with thanksgiving : for it is sanctified by the Word of GOD and prayer." Matter is not evil ; every created thing from GOD is good—" GOD saw everything that He had made, and, behold, it was very good ",

Genesis i. 31 ; it is not to be " refused ", but " received "—and that " with thanksgiving ". The food is even brought within a holy category by reason of the Word used in the prayer of thanksgiving, by being acknowledged as GOD's gift, and partaken of as nourishing the life for GOD's service—" We thank Thee for Thy good gift of this food. Bless it to our use, and us in Thy service ". Grace before meat seems to have been the practice in I Samuel ix. 13 ; our Lord blessed the loaves, Matthew xiv. 19 ; Paul gave thanks for the ship's meal in Acts xxvii. 35. In such company we may well maintain the custom ; and don't forget that " saying grace " in public can often be a very real bit of Christian testimony. Perhaps the significant word in all this rejoinder is that in verse 3, about " know the truth ", where the " know " is the strongest possible form of the word in the Greek =" *fully* know ". The full acquaintance with " the Scripture of Truth ", Daniel x. 21, is the sure antidote to the poison of the Father of Lies, John viii. 44. Let us get to know and to use this Word, and by it combat and conquer Satan, and his emissaries, as our Saviour always did. And here let us turn from all this cautionary ministry that is to be ours as well as Timothy's ; and see next—

A COUNSEL—TO BE STRONG

Which is the subject of verses 6–8. There are, alas, many weak Christians, but that ought to be a contradiction in terms —the Bible records many instances of such weaklings, but it leaves us in no doubt that it disapproves of them, makes no excuse for them. Indeed, all the teaching is on the other side. Right away back in Joshua i. 6, 7, 9, 18, it is " Be strong . . . only be strong . . . Have not I commanded thee, Be strong . . . only be strong . . ." In Haggai ii. 4, to leaders and to people, it is " Be strong . . . be strong . . . be strong ". In I Corinthians xvi. 13, it is " Be strong ". In Ephesians vi. 10, it is, " Finally, my brethren, be strong ". There it is, then, the oft repeated exhortation, to soldier, to leader, to worker, to believer—be strong. This is not an expectation for the few, it is expected of all ; GOD has no other purpose and proposal for His people than that they be robust in Christian stamina—strong enough to stand up to the blasts of temptation, strong enough to lend an arm to others on the road, strong enough to do solid hard work for GOD, strong enough to engage victoriously in the battle of the Lord, strong enough to grow still stronger day by day. Such is GOD's ideal for us. And if for us ordinary folk, how much more for those who are called to the superintendency of the saints—they, like Timothy, will need a special measure of this healthful, virile constitution, that they themselves may stand firm and upright, and that they may help others to stand. So our passage speaks of " nourished " in verse 6, and " exercise thyself " in verse 7.

The bishop is reminded, the " brethren " are to be reminded, that there are contributory causes of good health. One is *Good Nourishment*—" nourished up in the words of faith and of good doctrine, whereunto thou hast attained " : the tense of the verb " nourished " suggests that it is not by one outstanding banquet, nor by an occasional feast, but by a regular diet of everyday feeding on good solid fare—not, be it noted, fancy pastries but honest bread and butter, perhaps with a little jam ! " The words of faith and of good doctrine "—I fear that, as an article of diet, doctrine is out of fashion these days. We are so enamoured of the " pastries " of bright, brief, and brotherly addresses, or, as the case may be, of short, sweet, and sisterly talks, that we are impatient of anything the least bit " heavy ", as we think it. The consequence is that we are breeding a race of half-starved Christians. You can't grow strong on a glass of milk and a bun ! " Whereunto thou hast attained "—oh, so Timothy has himself acquired the sensible habit of good meals. Yes, from childhood upwards, II Timothy iii. 15. He is a young man of poor physical constitution, but there will be little to complain of in his spiritual stamina, because he has known and practised the secret of sound nourishment—the strong " meat " which was beyond the delicate digestion of the Corinthian Christians, I Corinthians iii.2.

So we come to another health hint, which is *Discerning Appetite* —" refuse profane and old wives' fables ". We recall, in II Peter i. 16, that " we have not followed cunningly devised fables, when we made known unto you . . . our Lord JESUS CHRIST " —not frauds, nor fables, nor fancies, but facts : plain, well-established facts on which our feet can rest and on which our souls can feed. If we desire to be really strong—for GOD and for others—there are certain foods that we shall " refuse ". The old-wives tales of insidious untruth are often clever counterfeits of the truth, but must on no account be " received ". Mark v. 24 says, " Take heed what ye hear ", and Luke viii. 18, " Take heed how ye hear " : we may take them as signifying the importance of taking good care both what, and how, we eat. Nothing could be more weighty for the well-being, and welfare, of a Christian than the nature and amount of his spiritual provender, and that he know what to enjoy and what to avoid.

Take another secret, of great value, namely, *Strenuous Exercise* —" Exercise thyself unto godliness. For bodily exercise profiteth little : but godliness is profitable unto all things, having promise of the life that now is, and of that which is to come ". What he says about bodily exercise is not to be taken as any disparagement of it : " little " should be " a little "—within its own limits, it is of value, for preserving health, and increasing strength, and even multiplying usefulness, rendering a man more capable of giving help in a case of hard need, and even of saving life. Oh yes, it is a good thing ; don't overdo it, don't make a fetish of it, don't let it so absorb your interest that you lose all concern for other and more important things—on the other hand, don't despise nor neglect it. A fit body is a fine boon. Ah, but greater, far greater still is fitness of soul. " Godliness is profitable "— not for a few things, but for all ; not for this short time here, but for all eternity hereafter. There is nothing secular that a man has to do that cannot—indeed should not—be better done because he is a godly man. He should be a better clerk than the worldling, a better workman, a better teacher, a better employer, a better servant. The late Dr. Alfred Plummer, of Durham, prince among Biblical expositors, put it this way, " A man who is formed, reformed, and informed by religion will do far more effectual work in the world than the same man without religion ". There ought to be a something, a touch, about all that he does that will stamp it as of the highest quality, in " all things "— secular as well as sacred. In Genesis xxxix. 2, we are told that " the LORD was with Joseph "—that constituted him a man of godliness. In the very next verse, it says, " His master saw that the LORD was with him "—I suppose it was something about the way in which he did his work, that something which godliness should always contribute. As to its profitableness, the record has it that " he was a prosperous man "—or, as old John Wycliffe translated it, " he was a luckie fellowe " : indeed, " the LORD made all that he did to prosper in his hand ". There it is again— the connection of the profitableness of godliness with " all things ". Moreover the range of this prosperity extends to the life that is to come. All the moral muscle and spiritual sinew that this " exercise " produces pays handsome dividends in eternity. Let us then adopt the daily exercises of the Means of Grace, the Earnest Service, and the Practice of the Presence.

There is one requisite that Paul does not mention here in

connection with good spiritual vitality, and that is *Pure Air*—
but he has already dealt with that, as seen in our fourth Study.
Let it be but briefly included at this point for the journey up
the hill, to breathe the refreshing atmosphere of the mountain
top of prayer will do much for the strengthening of the one who
habitually resorts thither. Archbishop Trench's lines come to
mind—

> " We kneel how weak ; we rise, how full of power.
> Why, therefore, do we do ourselves this wrong,
> And others—that we are not always strong ? "

And a Greater than he has said it that " they that wait upon the
LORD shall renew their strength ", Isaiah xl. 31. The gymnasium
of godliness is, for the most part, an open-air stadium where the
fresh breezes of the heavenly heights play upon the soul, em-
powering it for the exciting demands of the mounting life, or
for the exacting call of the running life, or for the exceeding
humdrum of the everyday walking life. Well, there they are,
the secrets of the strong—good food, good exercise, good air ;
and so we return to our passage for—

A CHALLENGE—TO BELIEVE

Which the concluding verses, 9–11, bring before us. " We
trust in the living GOD " : that is the very crux of the whole
matter, of this as of every aspect of the Christian life. It is
the initial act, which secures for us our eternal salvation from the
CHRIST who died ; it is the continual attitude, which secures
for us our diurnal supply of the resurrection power of the living
CHRIST. Let the word arrest your attention, my reader : Have
you, thus, put your trust in the Saviour ; and if so, are you,
as now a Christian, are you daily putting your trust in Him for
all the power you need ?

Of course, this practical trust has repercussions, some of which
are seen here. *The Effect of Belief*—" we labour . . . because
we trust ". The faith that does not set us to work is a poor,
feeble thing. James calls it a " dead " thing, James ii. 20.

> " I will not work my soul to save,
> For that my Lord has done ;
> But I will work like any slave.
> For love of His dear Son."

We are almost tempted to wonder whether an idle Christian is a Christian at all. There is so much to be done ; there are so few to do it ; there is so little time left ; there is so compelling an incentive, " for the love of CHRIST constraineth us ", II Corinthians v. 14. *The Aspect of Belief*—here mentioned : " we suffer . . . because we trust ". At least, Paul did. You have only to read II Corinthians xi. 23–8 to see how much he suffered for his faith. Sometimes, as I read those verses, I am filled with shame that I have suffered so little for my trust in Him. Are we ready if needs be to suffer reproach, or shame, or loss, or ridicule, or anything, for His Name ? There is a challenge for us all. *The Object of Belief*—" we trust in the living GOD ". The force of the Greek preposition is much stronger than the English, and means, " we set our hope on " ; also in I John iii. 3. Not in ourselves does our confidence rest ; nor in any other person, church, or ceremony ; but in Him, the Living One, the Saviour—potentially, " of all men " ; actually, " of those that believe ".

In all this guidance we ourselves heartily rejoice. What of the young Overseer, to whom it was written, " these things command and teach " ? How thankful he must have been. as he took up the superintendency of the Ephesian work that such leading and learning was passed on to him by the one to whom of all men he owed so much, and whom he loved so dearly.

VIII

A YOUNG MAN'S QUALIFICATIONS
FOR LEADERSHIP

I TIMOTHY iv. 12–16

12 Let no man despise thy youth ; but be thou an example of the believers, in word, in conversation, in charity, in spirit, in faith, in purity.

13 Till I come, give attendance to reading, to exhortation, to doctrine.

14 Neglect not the gift that is in thee, which was given thee by prophecy, with the laying on of the hands of the presbytery.

15 Meditate upon these things ; give thyself wholly to them ; that thy profiting may appear to all.

16 Take heed unto thyself, and unto the doctrine ; continue in them : for in doing this thou shalt both save thyself, and them that hear thee.

CONSTANTLY throughout the course of this Letter the writer has been pointing out to his beloved reader things that will make for the better discharge of the onerous duties now devolving upon him as he takes up the great and grave responsibility of guiding the young churches over which he has been set in the LORD ; but in this passage Paul gathers up the whole gamut of graces that Timothy will need for such a position. Five verses are here ; and each verse contains one such qualification for leadership. As youth takes the helm, he will find himself well equipped if he possess these characteristics.

First, we have *A Fertility of Character*, in verse 12. He is a " youth ", of about thirty-five—young indeed for such an eminent position ; his great mentor is, by contrast, " Paul the aged ", Philemon 9—a man, at about sixty-five, prematurely old from all his sufferings and adventures with the Gospel. Thus Timothy is to offset the fewness of his years by the richness of his character, so that his flock will quickly forget how young he is by their recognition of how godly he is—for he is to be " an example of the believers ", " of ", not " to " : that is, a pattern of what a believer ought to be, (i) " *In word* "—by his speech, the things he says, the way he says them ; " verbal intercourse of every kind ", as Vincent puts it. How enormously important this is, for words are seeds, whether of tares or wheat. (ii) " *In conversation* "—in the Elizabethan sense of the word : not talk, but walk, or daily behaviour. The world keenly watches a professing Christian to see how he behaves, and judges accordingly. Especially is this the case with a leader. Not just what he says, but what he does, and above all, what he is : that is the test. (iii) " *In charity* "—that is, love : literally the strongest power in the world, the sweetest thing in human experience. Thank GOD for that wonderful promise of Romans v. 5, " The love of GOD is shed abroad in our hearts by the HOLY GHOST who is given unto us "—it is possible for every Christian, seeing that they have the HOLY SPIRIT in them, Romans viii. 9, to have a heart full of love—for GOD and for their fellows. Oh, for a baptism of love—in leaders, and in led—in these days as in the first days of power. (iv) " *In Spirit* "—it is doubtful whether MS. authority will allow us to retain this in the list. If we do, I wonder if we may say that it will mean enthusiasm ? A quality strangely lacking from the make-up of many Christians. Plenty of enthusiasm for a football match, or for an election campaign, but so little of it for the service of GOD. How the magnificent enthusiasm of the Christian Scientists, the Jehovah's Witnesses, the Communists, should put us to shame. Oh, for flaming zeal again that once the church knew. This fine spirit will greatly help Timothy as he seeks to consolidate the position, and to advance the line (v) " *In faith* "—here, I think, is the meaning of faithfulness. That early church had much opposition to face, much danger threatening, much suffering to endure—and therefore much temptation to give up. The bishop would himself sometimes be discouraged, disappointed, distressed. Let him prove a pattern to his flock, in spite of everything, to keep on keeping on. (vi) " *In purity* "—not only in the moral significance of the word, though that of course ; but in the more general connotation : purity of motive as well as of action. Shall we say, practical holiness ? What a catena of fruits is here displayed, to enlarge and to enliven the character of any young man destined for leadership.

Second, we notice, and it has already been touched on, *A Fidelity of Ministry*, in verse 13. " Till I come "—Paul is hoping to visit Ephesus again sometime, and meanwhile he would have his young comrade carry on with the work, not losing opportunities, nor losing heart. What an echo is this of the Saviour's " Till I come ", in Luke xix. 13, who bids us " occupy ", carry on the business, until He returns to take over. The ministry in this verse of ours is divided up into three main activities. (i) *The " reading "*—which means here, I imagine, the public reading of the Scriptures. One thinks of the Master, who, " as His custom was, went into the synagogue on the Sabbath day, and stood up for to read ", Luke iv. 16. How important this ministry is ; and how highly privileged is the man who is allowed thus to read the Word in the ears of the people, as Ezra did from his " pulpit of wood ", Nehemiah viii. 3–4, when " all the people were attentive unto the book ". Following this Old Testament scribe and his helpers, let all readers aspire to their efficiency, who " read . . . distinctly, and gave the sense, and caused them to understand the reading ", verse 8. Then comes (ii) *The " exhortation "*—some word of guidance, of rebuke, of comfort, of challenge, arising out of the words read. The church members of those early days, no less than the congregations of to-day, are in real need of such inspiriting utterances. Life is so difficult, beset by such perplexities and anxieties ; and the Bible is so germane to life, whether ancient or modern, always so up to date, so relevant to the situation, so adequate to any call upon it. One wonders that this Scriptural exhortation is not infrequently disregarded in these days, in favour of " that which satisfieth not ", Isaiah lv. 2. Ye modern Timothys, keep close to your Bibles, and exhort therefrom. And (iii) *The " doctrine "*—the teaching, of which we spoke just now. When JESUS ministered in the synagogues of Galilee, a distinction was noted between His " preaching " and " teaching ", Matthew iv. 23. Whatever was the need for the specialised instruction of that latter word in those days, the necessity to-day is greatly aggravated. The abysmal ignorance now obtaining in the world, and amazingly enough even in our churches, is such as to constitute a clamant call for a teaching ministry. May we soon get back to it ; and—Timothy !—don't you ever lose it. He is to give close and constant attention, then, to reading, to exhortation, to doctrine, and thus to show a happy fidelity in his ministry.

Third, we get *A Felicity of Gift*, in verse 14. We must bear in mind (i) *The position*—which Timothy occupied, as the human director of the life of that group of churches, gathered about the River Cayster, bearing the onus of matters personal, ecclesiastical, doctrinal, moral, practical. To have such a charge was no mean burden—especially on young shoulders. To discharge a bishopric to-day must be an enormously onerous occupation, which would fill us lesser folk with dismay. In that pristine age of the church, one imagines that it would be not less but perhaps more heavy, for there was no precedent to follow, no experience to guide ; all the while they were blazing the trail. Ah, but there was a happy circumstance thereto belonging (ii) *The power*—many-sided, and all-sufficient for all the occurrences, and opportunities, and oppositions that might arise. This power was in the form of a " gift "—not in the sense in which we say that a man is naturally gifted, but in the meaning that a particular gift was specially provided for an exceptional purpose. We further note that this donation was not a mere influence, nor a thing of any kind, but actually a Person, none other than the HOLY SPIRIT Himself. This does not imply that Timothy did not previously have Him, since he would not be a Christian if he had not, for " if any man have not the SPIRIT of CHRIST he is none of His ", Romans viii. 9 ; but there is, apart from this permanent abiding of Him in the believer's heart, a specific anointing of the SPIRIT for specific service. This is what Timothy had received ; the power is there for the taking—just as the electric current is there in your house, but can only be of use if you switch it on ; so is this leader of the Christian forces endowed, imbued, with the all-powerful Current, but only the movement of the switch of faith can procure for the using the light, and warmth, and power required. He is, indeed, exhorted " neglect not the Gift that is in thee ". There lies the secret of the low level of some Christian life, the powerlessness of some Christian service : the Current is there, but the Switch is neglected. See a clear instance of this in I Corinthians vi. 19, " What ? know ye not that . . . the HOLY GHOST is in you ? " Those believers were living in a deeply unworthy fashion, uncleanness was rife amongst them—yet, the Holy One was in them, they *ought not* to be unholy ; and they *need not* be unholy. The power was there ; but they, for whatever reason, neglected to let Him in, to set Him free, to do the work that He is so able, so willing, and so eager to do. So Timothy, so Christian—is it the Light of guidance you want, is it the Warmth of love you seek, is it the Power for service you crave ? It is all there, GOD's " gift " to you—let nothing prevent your turning on the switch, that so your need and His great fulness meet. Just a word about (iii) *The prophecy*—" given thee by prophecy, with the laying on of the hands of the presbytery ". It would seem that in those beginning days, as in the succeeding years, the rite of the laying on of hands was accompanied by the preaching of the Word. For I think that the word " prophecy ", which has two meanings in different parts of Scripture, is used here not in its sense of fore-telling, but forth-telling. The telling forth of some Word of GOD as a strength and encouragement to the one being set apart. So was Timothy commissioned by the HOLY GHOST, the outward sign and symbol whereof was this laying on of hands. Barnabas and Saul, himself, had been sent forth in the same manner, Acts xiii. 3. Note that it is here said to have been by the hands of the presbytery, as in essence in Paul's own case ; but in II Timothy i. 6 Paul declares that it was " by the putting on of my hands ". There is no contradiction here : evidently both Paul and the representatives of the presbyterate each took part in the solemn act of consecration. That moment of the separating sign (see Romans i. 1) must have been one of the most moving occasions in this young man's experience ; and the apostle would have him never forget it, never " neglect " it. How felicitous is the Gift.

Fourth, we observe a *Fixity of Purpose*, in verse 15. Consider (i) *The practice*—that is enjoined, " Meditate upon these things ". Some of the translators reject the word, and prefer to render it, be diligent in, or practise ; but there seems no real reason why we should not preserve the choice of the Authorised Version, the scholars do not positively reject it. After all, what a fine habit is meditation. Psalm i. 1-2 says that he is a happy man who " in His law doth . . . meditate " ; and even as far back as Joshua i. 8, that young warrior is recommended, as part of his soldierly well-being, to give such earnest attention to the Book as to " meditate therein " ; and now this New Testament young successor, engaged upon battle of another sort, is urged likewise to " meditate ". The word suggests the idea of the ruminant animal chewing the cud—having found his toothsome morsel, and, for the lasting taste of it. and the better digestion of it, turns it over and over. Spiritually, the Christian's mouth is his mind ; and just as, in Joshua's case, " this book of the law shall not depart out of thy mouth ", but thou shalt retain it there and " chew " it over, so the believer, having discovered his succulent portion of GOD's words and works, is not to let it slip hastily away, but is to retain it and turn it over in his mind, that he may the longer sample its delight, for " How sweet are Thy words unto my taste ! yea, sweeter than honey to my mouth ! " Psalm cxix. 103 ; and that he may the better " inwardly digest " it, as our Church of England Advent collect puts it. No wonder that the same Psalmist, in his 97th verse, says, " It is my meditation all the day ". Timothy, then, is to dwell

" upon these things " that GOD has done, and is prepared to do, even for him. All which is emphasised by what is said, next, of (ii) *The pre-occupation*—" give thyself wholly to them ". In other words, he is to throw himself completely into his ministry —his mind, and mouth, and members, all at it, and always at it ; all in, so far as his personality is concerned : all out, so far as his activity is concerned. The late John Morley tells us, in his biography of the great Prime Minister, that when W. E. Gladstone was asked, as he often was, for the secret of his success-ful life, he always replied in one word, " Concentration ". This " give thyself wholly to them " is, literally, " be in them "— become entirely wrapped up in them. One recalls that intriguing description of the old prophet as " the LORD's messenger in the LORD's message ", Haggai i. 13—that's it : as if he had made it so much a part of himself that his whole soul was in it, as if man and message, message and man, were united as one thing. And with Timothy, as if man and ministry, ministry and man, were one, so completely identified was he with " these things ". There is such a thing as legitimate rest and recreation—and I plead that, even for the work's sake, apart from anything else, a place shall be found for the lighter side of life. All work and no play makes even Christian Jack a dull boy. But so far as the general tenor of life is concerned, let us make sure that we deal firmly with anything that will distract us from the main purpose of a Christian life—which is, to serve GOD and to save souls. Having mentioned Mr. Gladstone, it is strange that Benjamin Disraeli, his implacable political foe, had for his lode-star, Per-sistency of Purpose. Two famous Prime Ministers. Another Prime Minister, more famous still, seems to have had very much the same motto, for I read that " Daniel purposed . . . and Daniel continued ", Daniel i. 8, 21. Stickability is an essential quality for effective leadership. Following which, ponder (iii) *The progress*—" that thy profiting may appear to all ". The word " profiting " means growth, advance, progress ; and leaders, as well as led, must ever be moving onward and upward. And it will be found that the two characteristics we have just mentioned are as the two feet upon which the movement is made—the one, thoughtful penetration into the past, with all its encouragement and inspiration ; the other, purposeful concentration on the present, with all its duties and demands. Thus will " appear ", obvious to all, in Timothy's case, or in ours, a welcome growth in power, in grace, in influence, in fruit-fulness. So let it be with us as with David, " O GOD, my heart is fixed ", Psalm cviii. 1—for if it be thus it will give fixity to all our life, and endeavour.

Fifth, we come to a *Faculty of Continuance*, in verse 16. We have spoken of fixity of purpose, and now we dwell on the thought of continuance in that purpose. But first we mark *the combination*—" Take heed unto thyself, and unto the doctrine ". The order seems right, doesn't it ? First the teacher is to be right ; and then the teaching is to be right—the man must be up to standard first as a person and then as a pedagogue. The phrase " take heed " has a deeply important meaning—it does not signify just a passing glance, a cursory thought, but, to give it its literal translation, it is " fasten thy attention on ". This implies earnest examination, a really genuine attempt to get, and keep, things in proper condition. What am I like ? What is my work like ? How am I progressing in grace ? How is my work growing in power ? Will I stand up to the divine scrutiny ? Will my work pass muster in His eyes ? If in II Corinthians xiii. 5 we are told " Examine yourselves ", the best way to do that is to ask GOD to do it for us, " Examine me, O LORD, and prove me ", Psalm xxvi. 2. It may be a painful and humiliating process ; but, in the result, it will be infinitely worth while. Let there be a regular submitting of ourselves and our service to the searching test of the HOLY SPIRIT. Most people go to a doctor when they feel ill ; but I have a friend who, like some others, goes habitually to his doctor for a thorough overhaul every year. I imagine that to be a very sensible practice, physically ; I know it is a very sensible thing spiritually—only, I suggest, more frequently than once a year. On one occasion I gave an address to some children on " Get straight, Keep straight, Make straight " : a few days afterwards, one of my little hearers, aged six, went to his mother, and so seriously asked, " Mummie, am I going straight ? " That's it : to make the plan of going regularly to the HOLY SPIRIT, who is so ready to help, and ask Him the all-important question, " Am I going straight ? " If we really do want to know, and if we really do desire to put anything right that is wrong, He will make it plain. " If any man will [wills to] do His will, He shall know . . ." said the Master Himself, in John vii. 17. So let the Christian leader " take heed " to keep short accounts with GOD, to keep all the while up to the mark. And now comes (ii) *The continuation*—" continue in them ". The beginning of things can be, at times, comparatively easy : it is the keeping them up that is the problem. The freshness, the excitement, helps us to start : it is the humdrum sameness that so often tempts us to stop. The believers of the Galatian churches found from experience this difficulty of going on—" Ye did run well; who did hinder you ? " Galatians v. 7. On the other hand, those first believers, of Acts ii. 42, had discovered some grand secrets for the persistent life in the assiduous use of the public means of grace. " They continued stedfastly in the apostles' doctrine, and [the] fellowship, and in [the] breaking of bread, and in [the] prayers "—the definite article is in all the places in the Greek; and that is why I think I am justified in characterising these as *public* means of grace. Greatly daring, I venture to render them as the early equivalents of such helps as the Bible School, the Church Socials, the Lord's Table, and the Prayer Meeting. If we make a point of trying to draw the newborn Christians into such gatherings, I believe we shall find a great many more of them continuing. Let them find, not, as so often, a frigid acknowledgment, but a warm welcome to the church circle, and they are much more likely to settle down, and to " stick "—not all, perhaps, but a larger number than otherwise might do so. It is a weakness—and one that is difficult to remedy—that in some Gospel campaigns, many professing converts so soon backslide, owing to their not being helped to form a definite church connection. This, as I have said, is often very hard to bring about; but it is greatly to be desired that we should take all possible pains to get such young believers linked up with some body of Christians. The Pentecost " results " were numerically large—" about three thousand "; but apparently none drifted away—why ? Because of their adherence to those spiritual exercises. The bishop and his flock must " continue in them ". Lastly, we have (iii) *The culmination*—" thou shalt both save thyself, and them that hear thee ". What greater joy can come to any rank of minister, any kind of Christian, than, being saved himself, to have been GOD's instrument in saving others through the testimony he has been able to give. So do we end our study of these qualifications of leadership, thus earnestly pressed by Paul, and, doubtless, so eminently possessed by Timothy—who will have learned that he cannot lead others unless he himself first tread the road ahead. Do not Oliver Goldsmith's lines, in his " Deserted Village ", beautifully put the point, in the example of the village parson, who—

> " . . . as a bird each fond endearment tries
> To tempt its new-fledged offspring to the skies,
> He tried each art, reproved each dull delay,
> Allured to brighter worlds and led the way."

Yet there was a time when Paul himself dictated the poignant lines of I Corinthians ix. 27, " . . . lest that by any means, when I have preached to others, I myself should be a castaway [cast aside] "—not a " cast out ", for the apostle would know of the Saviour's promise, " him that cometh to Me I will in no wise [the Greek behind this negative is so strong " not on any account "] cast out ", John vi. 37 ; neither a " cast off ", for he will be familiar with the principle applied by JEHOVAH to His own, " Hath GOD cast away His people ? " Romans xi. 1. No, not these ; but a dread possibility for even the keenest of believers, if he become unwatchful, a " cast aside ". Like that fountain-pen in the drawer of your desk, that was bought with a price, that was presented to you, that served you so well but that has gone wrong and is no longer usuable—it is still yours, it is still kept safe for a sentimental reason, but it is now derelict. Many a man who once was prominent in Christian service, who did great work for GOD, is now, alas, on the shelf, no longer usable, through slackening of vigilance. The words are to be taken as a solemn warning to all followers : but what shall be said of leaders—except doubly to underline the same thought. If Paul's eyes were open to it, may ours be also—and all our whole body, as in Romans vi. 13 and xii. 1, be ever, and daily, kept by Him and for Him.

IX

SOCIAL ASPECTS

I TIMOTHY v. 1–16; vi. 1–2

1 Rebuke not an elder, but intreat *him* as a father ; *and* the younger men as brethren ;

2 The elder women as mothers ; the younger as sisters, with all purity.

3 Honour widows that are widows indeed.

4 But if any widow have children or nephews, let them learn first to shew piety at home, and to requite their parents : for that is good and acceptable before God.

5 Now she that is a widow indeed, and desolate, trusteth in God, and continueth in supplications and prayers night and day.

6 But she that liveth in pleasure is dead while she liveth.

7 And these things give in charge, that they may be blameless.

8 But if any provide not for his own, and specially for those of his own house, he hath denied the faith, and is worse than an infidel.

9 Let not a widow be taken into the number under threescore years old, having been the wife of one man.

10 Well reported of for good works ; if she have brought up children, if she have lodged strangers, if she have washed the saints' feet, if she have relieved the afflicted, if she have diligently followed every good work.

11 But the younger widows refuse : for when they have begun to wax wanton against Christ, they will marry ;

12 Having damnation, because they have cast off their first faith.

13 And withal they learn *to be* idle, wandering about from house to house ; and not only idle, but tattlers also and busybodies, speaking things which they ought not.

14 I will therefore that the younger women marry, bear children, guide the house, give none occasion to the adversary to speak reproachfully.

15 For some are already turned aside after Satan.

16 If any man or woman that believeth have widows, let them relieve them, and let not the church be charged ; that it may relieve them that are widows indeed.

1 Let as many servants as are under the yoke count their own masters worthy of all honour, that the name of God and *his* doctrine be not blasphemed.

2 And they that have believing masters, let them not despise *them*,

87

because they are brethren ; but rather do *them* service, because they are faithful and beloved, partakers of the benefit. These things teach and exhort.

THE Christian religion is essentially a personal thing. It comes to individuals, who, to adapt the old prophet, are " gathered one by one " ; but those individuals will not be long in the faith before they begin to realise that their religion has all kinds of social implications, in regard to their own homes, in regard to their fellow Christians, in regard to their work, and in regard to the world at large. Indeed, James i. 27 will tell them that " pure religion and undefiled before GOD and the Father is this, to visit the fatherless and widows in their affliction, and to keep himself unspotted from the world "—wherein is his obligation to " himself ", but also that towards those needy others. The Epistle to the Romans, pre-eminently the doctrinal epistle, leading up to the Great Surrender, in xii. 1, goes on to deal in most practical fashion with the surrendered one's duties towards others. The Epistle to the Ephesians, having in its earlier chapters considered the high theme of " the heavenlies ", comes down later into the earthlies, to show to us the Ideal Home Exhibition, in the proper Christian relationships between husbands and wives, parents and children, masters and servants. There is no question that, in the mind of the HOLY SPIRIT, who inspired these utterances, the social aspects of the faith are of fundamental importance. Working all this out in terms of the particular necessities of the area of Timothy's jurisdiction—the under-pastors of the local churches, and the pastor-in-chief, are here guided accordingly.

THE SPIRITUAL MEMBERS OF THE FAMILY ; AND HOW TO TREAT THEM

We have this indicated in our verses 1–2 ; and we note at once the word " family " in this sub-title, for it is used so often in the New Testament, to describe the members of the Christian group. The group is named under so many figures—soldiers in the army, limbs in the body, competitors in the race, servants in the household, singers in the choir, branches in the vine ; but the most frequent is this as members of the family—being born, newborn, into it by the SPIRIT. Every real Christian is a child of the Father, and is consequently intimately related to all the other children. That fact—not just fancy, or figure, but fact—should govern our behaviour towards all our fellows in CHRIST. I wonder

if it does ? Here, then, is the rule : (a) *The old men* of the family
are to be treated as fathers—the youthful bishop is not to deal
with them as he would the younger ones ; not to " rebuke "
them for a fault, but rather to " intreat " them to do better.
(b) *The young men* of the family are to be treated as brothers—
their leaders are not to put on " airs " of superiority : let their
character be superior, and their position perchance, but let
their behaviour be brotherly. (c) *The old women* of the family
are to be treated as mothers—giving them all the esteem, affection, and help that the maternal relationship should always evoke.
(d) *The young women* of the family are to be treated as sisters
—and guarded from all unchaste thought, and unholy attention.
One's recollection goes at once to John's similar delineation of
the varying status of the members of the Christian family, in
I John ii. 12–14, as—" little children ", those who have only
just been born again ; " young men ", those who are strong,
virile, and adventurous in the faith ; " fathers ", those who have
longer knowledge of Him, and who have begotten sons in the
Gospel—even as Paul had begotten Timothy, " my own son ",
I Timothy i. 2 ; " my dearly beloved son ", II Timothy i. 2.
Only, let us seek to be up to standard at each stage of our growth
—which is what " perfect " means, in such a verse as Matthew
v. 48. Only, let us treat the other members of the spiritual family
in this becoming way. Next—

THE SUFFERING MEMBERS OF THE FAMILY ; AND HOW TO HELP THEM

This is unfolded in verses 3–8, and in verse 16. It is concerned
with those who are described as " widows indeed "—not merely
ladies who have been bereaved of their husbands, but bereft of
all ! Seeing that, in these earliest days of Christianity, a big
proportion of the believers were of the poorer people, it would be
a not uncommon thing that a woman who lost her husband and
his earnings would be in just such a condition as is here contemplated. It may well be hoped that there will be those of
her own family, or those of the family of the church, who will
rally round her, and see that she is cared for, and adequately
provided for. So we observe, first (i) *The relations' responsibility
for widows*—verse 4 says that " children or nephews . . . [are]
to requite their parents : for that is good and acceptable before
GOD ". It is sad to see so many cases, in these days, of sons and
daughters who seem to resent their responsibilities for looking

after the welfare of their aged parents : it is so ungracious and ungrateful a way to " requite " them for all that they have done for, and been to, their children since they were little things, and right on through the intervening years. How grievous a thing this is in GOD's eyes. Indeed, " if any provide not for his own . . . he hath denied the faith "—his belief has told him to do this, and he has refused, and said " No " ; " and is worse than an infidel "—for this latter man does not know any better, while the believer sins against the light. Sin is always worse in a Christian than in a non-Christian, for this reason. Paul, when writing to the young people of Timothy's congregations, reminds them of that promise-bearing section of the old, universal, moral law, " Honour thy father and mother ; which is the first commandment with promise ", Ephesians vi. 2. GOD gives a special blessing to those who thus care for the old people ; and we have seen that fulfilled over and over again. On the whole, the duty was honourably observed in Old Israel ; but even there we find exceptions, as stated by our Lord Himself in Mark vii. 10–12, " Moses said, Honour thy father and thy mother . . . but ye say, If a man shall say to his father or mother, It is Corban, that is to say, a gift, by whatsoever thou mightest be profited by me ; he shall be free. And ye suffer him no more to do ought for his father or his mother "—an insufferable evasion of plain, and GOD-ordered, duty, allowed, perhaps even encouraged, by those scribes and Pharisees. To illustrate : here is a man of means who jibs at providing for his parents ; he puts aside the money to be a Gift (Corban) for the Temple, on his decease ; that is to excuse him from his obligation to his parents—they cannot benefit by that money, because it is already " booked " for the Temple funds and he is thenceforth released from his duty. Incidentally, there was nothing to prevent his using that money for himself during his lifetime : but his parents must go without ! What a situation ; and how indignant our Lord was. Timothy is to see that his flock is made aware of GOD's will in this matter of social obligation, ard to make sure that the duty is not evaded. It is a sad reflection on some types of human nature that all this stress and emphasis on the matter should be called for. See next (ii) *The churches' responsibility for widows indeed*—the not only bereaved, but bereft. The first thing is that they are to be " honoured ", verse 3, not looked down on because they are poor. It is what a person is, not what he has, that is the proper gauge of honour, or of dishonour—and these desolate women are to be esteemed as proud, not pauper, ladies. For let it not be forgotten that each belongs in truth to the aristocracy of grace, for she "trusteth in GOD, and continueth in supplications and prayers night and day", verse 5, their attitude was ever towards GOD, and their appetite was always for the things of GOD. So different from the one that "liveth in pleasure", who is all for seeing life, not realising, poor thing, that, so far as satisfaction is concerned, her life is completely dead. To have pleasure in life is a legitimate, and healthy thing; but to live for pleasure, as some people do, and did even in Timothy's day, is an unworthy, and unhealthy, thing. The difference between Christians is largely a matter of appetite—is he satisfied, with the things of GOD, or does he hanker after the things of the world? There lies the distinction between the first-class Christian and the third. There was no doubt as to which class these troubled women belonged. By the way, GOD has never guaranteed that the Christian, even the first-class one, shall be immune from the "ills that flesh is heir to"; but He has promised His presence and help. From the oft-quoted Romans viii. 28 I draw the conclusion that, so far as we believers are concerned, if we implicitly trust His loving hand, though things may hurt, they never shall harm. Well now, while the "widows" are the responsibility of their relatives, "let . . . the church be charged, that it . . . relieve them that are widows indeed", verse 16. These have no one to look after them; but they are in the family, so the onus of their maintenance rests on the church. They are suffering members; therefore, according to I Corinthians xii. 26, "all the members suffer with" them, entering into their trials and needs, and seeking to "relieve" them.

There is one phrase here which, before passing on, I want to drag out of its context, because it contains a principle applying to Christian life in general. It is in verse 4—"learn first to shew piety at home". In its place here, it is the Scriptural way of saying that "charity begins at home"; but, in its wider application, it teaches us that all Christian life, virtue, or testimony should begin there. It is Exercise I, a mere ABC, in the curriculum of the school of CHRIST—"learn first". Some disciples of His seem to have by-passed that lesson, for the home is the very last place where the Christian spirit and behaviour are seen —lambs in the church, boors in the home: that is the way with some. How otherwise was it with the order of our Lord JESUS. When Legion was cured and converted, he was all for going overseas at once with the Master to bear witness to His wondrous work. A splendid idea; but the Lord had another idea—"Go

home to thy friends, and tell them how great things the Lord
hath done for thee ", Mark v. 19; " Return to thine own house,
and shew how great things GOD hath done unto thee ", Luke
viii. 39. The two Evangelists record each one of the two things
that the Saviour commanded—he was to " shew " the change,
and " tell " how it happened. And this, first of all, at home :
it was there that they had suffered most from his ill conduct :
they shall be the first to see, and appreciate, the " great " transformation and to hear of the Great Transformer Himself. Serve
Him in the mission-field, yes ; in the slums of the great city,
yes ; in Church and Sunday School, yes ; but first, first, first
—" learn first to shew piety at home ! " Think now of—

The Specialist Members of the Family ; and how to Choose Them

That we shall find in verses 9–15. Evidently in the Early
Church there was a special Order of Widows recruited for
specialist service. When a woman comes to widowhood, she
sometimes feels that the bottom has dropped out of life ; now
that her loved one has gone, she might herself just as well go ;
it was no longer worth living. To a widow in such a frame of
mind, if she were a Christian, one of the Family, it would come,
after her grief was a little assuaged, as a glad surprise to learn
that her life henceforth need not be the useless thing she had
surmised, that the conditions being fulfilled, she might join this
Order, and devote herself to some social ministry : her remaining
years might, after all, be, not only pleasurable to herself, but
profitable to others. How happily, and hopefully, she would
take up life again, and spend it afresh for good, and for GOD.
Bishop Timothy would know all about this Order, and doubtless
would be grateful to have Paul's guidance regarding it.

We consider, first (i) *Those to be admitted.* They are not to
" be taken into the number ", verse 9, that is, not to be enrolled
as a member, under sixty years old—that would normally ensure
that the woman would have a pretty wide experience of human
life, and a pretty fair judgment of the need and personality of
any who should apply for help. Beyond this, it appears that
quite high qualifications were demanded of those who were
elected to the Order. They must have a good report covering
a five fold activity in Christian social service (1) " *If she have
brought up children* "—the successful rearing of little ones is an
exacting occupation, and is a great test, both of ability, good

sense, moral character, sound discipline, and warm love. (2) " If *she have lodged strangers* "—the practice of Christian hospitality requires a certain good-heartedness and quiet management that will cope with the unexpected arrival of people needing lodgment for the while. (3) " *If she have washed the saints' feet* "—a service for others that no ordinary person would willingly undertake, but which JESUS did specifically for an example to His disciples, John xiii. 15. It is a work emanating only from a great humility, and a high sense of discipleship. (4) " *If she have relieved the afflicted* "—it was not a very sympathetic age, and sufferings of many sorts abounded, so that if any heart beat for another's ills, it had plenty of chances of offering relief. Hearts could pass stonily by at the sight of even deep distress, as in Luke x. 31–2 ; but these widows would, like their Saviour, be ever drawn by the need of the afflicted. Even if they could not do much, they would do what they could. (5) " *If she have diligently followed every good work* "—such is the summing up of this social Sister-hood. " Good works " are ever the test of healthy faith, as Ephesians ii. 10 makes plain, and as James ii. 17 brings home. These ladies had shown their faith, the livingness of their faith, by their works. Paul told that other chief-pastor, the Bishop of Crete, that " they which have believed in GOD . . . be careful to maintain good works ", Titus iii. 8. I am sure you will agree that membership of this Order of Widows required qualities of life and character of an unusually high degree.

When we turn aside to ponder (ii) *Those not to be admitted*—we take up verses 11–15 of our passage. If the conditions of inclusion were stringent, the rules for exclusion were not less strong. Paul leaves Timothy in no manner of doubt as to the sort of person that is unsuitable for this particular form of service.. The " younger widows ", the under-sixties, and much under, they are to " refuse ", verse 11. Such may in their first emotion of grief wish to dedicate their lives to this service ; but then their desire for CHRIST's service may cool down, and as opposed to that work of CHRIST they " wax wanton " with sexual desire, and wish to marry again, having condemnation (not " damna-tion ") for having " cast off their first faith ", or having broken their first pledge. That would be the danger of admitting some of the younger untried, unstable widows. Another thing, the restless-ness of such may lead to their spending their energies going around one another's houses, idling their time away, gossiping, slandering, and what not, verse 13. The best thing for them would be to marry again, to settle down, to bear children and to run a home. That is the life for them, not that other. Enough harm has been done already, for there has been given " occasion to the adversary to speak reproachfully, for some are already turned aside after Satan ", verses 14–15, who is only too anxious to lure Christians " after " himself and " against " CHRIST, verse 11. One further matter calls for our attention before passing from our main subject of the social aspects of Christianity.

THE SERVING MEMBERS OF THE FAMILY; AND HOW TO GUIDE THEM

For this we go over to chapter vi. and examine verses 1–2. These " servants " were, as the original word indicates, slaves. It is interesting to note that the institution of slavery is taken for granted. The rights, or wrongs, of the matter are not argued anywhere in the New Testament. Our Lord did not condemn nor abolish it—not then, though He has done so since. There is a right time for things, and a right method ; and the Master judged that the moment was not ripe, and also that a violent, revolutionary campaign was not the way to deal with this deep-seated practice. The gradual permeation of the spirit of CHRIST in the hearts of men has brought about the desirable change of outlook on this abhorrent evil. To the writer and reader of this Letter, then, slavery was an old-established and familiar thing ; and through the preaching of the Gospel a large number of the slaves had become real Christians.

Paul has something to say in respect of two classes of these serving members of the community. (i) *The Christian slaves of non-Christians*—these are to " count their own masters worthy of all honour ". That is to say, they are to render them full obedience. Do you remember how, in Matthew vi. 24, our Lord says, " No man can serve two masters "—but surely he can ! A gardener can work at three houses every week, and thus serve three masters. Yes, in our English sense of the word ; but in the Greek the word is a much stronger one, and the rendering should be, " No man can be a slave to two masters "—and that is patently true. A slave was the exclusive property of his owner, and was completely subservient to his orders, without any limit, or appeal. Now, says the apostle, the slave who is a Christian is to be particularly careful to render his master faithful, and good, service, " that the Name of GOD, and His doctrine, be not blasphemed ". If he is slack, or insubordinate, or careless, or in any way unsatisfactory, the heathen master will be sure to put it down to his religion. That is true of anyone who works in any serving capacity. He works under his master's eye, an eye all the more critical if he is a heathen and is on the look out for any cause to hold the Christian cause in disrepute. Christian young man or young woman, serving in an office, a factory, a workshop, a home—you bear a specially big responsibility, lest you bring dishonour on your Supreme Master's name because you serve your earthly master so ill. A Christian young fellow, while his master was out at lunch one day, was tempted by a commercial traveller to agree to some shady transaction. The man urged " Come on, your master's not in ". To which the lad very properly replied, his finger pointed upward, " Excuse me, my Master is always in ". Another aspect is introduced here in the case of (ii) *The Christian slaves of fellow-Christians*—these should not despise them because they are brethren ", should not take any advantage nor claim any indulgence because they are just as much Christians as their masters are. Rather should they make a point of giving all the better service because they both alike share in the title of " faithful and beloved " in the Lord, being fellow-partakers in that benefit, that boon, that blessing. Not the less are they their master's slaves, because they are both the Master's slaves. How suggestive is Paul's dealing with that now converted runaway slave, Onesimus, whom he sends back to his master, another convert of Paul's, to be " now profitable ", Philemon 11, as a slave, and, as now a Christian, a " brother beloved ", verse 16. Will Onesimus, through fear of legitimate punishment, fail to deliver the letter at the master's residence at Colossæ—will he, at the last mile, run away again ? Paul thought of that, and he arranged for him to travel with Tychicus, who carried the Epistle to the Colossians, and who had perhaps the whispered instructions that if Onesimus should panic, he was to be seen up to the very door of his duty. All imagination ? Yes, I dare say ! But if so, I still don't see why the church epistle should not have been taken by Onesimus as he was in any case going there.

How this very apostle rejoiced in regarding himself as " the servant [bond-slave] of JESUS CHRIST ", Romans i. 1—he gloried in being bound hand and foot to such a Master, sought no greater distinction than to bear in his body " the marks ", Galatians vi. 17, of the slave-branding of his Lord. As slave, he will have *no will of his own*—adopting words primarily referring to his Lord, he says, " I come to do Thy will ", Hebrews x. 9 ; Psalm xl. 7–8 ; he will have *no belongings of his own*—all that he has is His, at

His disposal and use ; he will have *no programme of his own*—he has but to find his Master's plans, and then to carry out His wishes ; he will have *no cares of his own*—the slave-owner assumes all responsibility for the protection and provision of his servant : his food, and clothes, and health, and shelter, all are seen to by him—and by Him ; he will have *no supplies of his own*—everything he needs for the due performance of his duties is provided ; " who goeth a warfare at his own charges ? " I Corinthians ix. 7, nor any slave produce his wherewithal, but " ye, always having all sufficiency in all things, may abound to every good work ", II Corinthians ix. 8. All these, and all else, are the Master's province : the slave's is only the dual onus to Trust and Obey.

X

REWARDS AND REBUKES

I TIMOTHY v. 17–25

17 Let the elders that rule well be counted worthy of double honour, especially they who labour in the word and doctrine.

18 For the scripture saith, Thou shalt not muzzle the ox that treadeth out the corn. And, The labourer *is* worthy of his reward.

19 Against an elder receive not an accusation, but before two or three witnesses.

20 Them that sin rebuke before all, that others also may fear.

21 I charge *thee* before God, and the Lord Jesus Christ, and the elect angels, that thou observe these things without preferring one before another, doing nothing by partiality.

22 Lay hands suddenly on no man, neither be partaker of other men's sins : keep thyself pure.

23 Drink no longer water, but use a little wine for thy stomach's sake and thine often infirmities.

24 Some men's sins are open beforehand, going before to judgment ; and some *men* they follow after.

25 Likewise also the good works *of some* are manifest beforehand ; and they that are otherwise cannot be hid.

THE word for " elders " here is the same as that in verse 1, but consideration of the contexts—always a matter of prime importance in the elucidation and exposition of Scripture—suggests that in the earlier passage it means elders in age, while here it is elders in position. In fact, it appears that Paul is giving guidance to Timothy, the Overseer, concerning the choosing and appointment of what we may call underseers, men charged with the leadership in the local churches. That must always be a matter of utmost, indeed vital, importance, for the spiritual quality of the congregation will largely (though not always, nor entirely) depend upon the character of their pastor. The apostle, then, here puts before the Pastor-in-Chief some matters, in general, and in particular, on the subject of those who occupy or who shall be called to occupy these strategic positions. First he deals with—

THE REWARD OF FAITHFUL LEADERS

What he has to say on this is contained in verses 17–18, and he begins by considering (i) *The estimate of their worth*—" let the elders that rule well be counted worthy ". *By men*—is the point of the passage. Of course, men cannot judge of a minister's motives, and of the inner secrets of his heart, though even of these a shrewd observer, or, better still, a saintly person, can often form a pretty accurate opinion—for these things will out. These apart, however, men do arrive at some judgment of a pastor's worthiness or unworthiness. Does he " rule well " ? That is a matter of outward observation, and his flock—and some outsiders—are in a position to get some idea of the real state of affairs. For example : Is he firm in decision, while being kindly in manner ? Is he a comfort to the older friends, while proving an inspiration to the young ? Is he faithful concerning sin, while tactful towards sinners ? Is he keen to win the outsider, while careful to build up those that are within ? Is he thoroughly spiritual, while at the same time entirely practical ? Is he a good preacher, while being a godly man ? How many of those tests were put concerning those early pastors, I don't know ; but they certainly are posed of his modern counterpart, for the present-day pastor is expected to be a positive paragon ! But if those pastors passed man's judgment, was that enough ; if they failed of man's judgment, was that final ? No ; for they must satisfy another examination. *By GOD*—is he also to be scrutinised. And that is, of course, the main thing : to be " counted worthy " by Him. It may so often happen that man's accountancy is reversed : the seemingly good man being accounted a failure, the man of little account being held in high regard—

> " Men heed thee, love thee, praise thee not,
> The Master praises—what are men ? "

Many a man has coveted a " V.C."—but wise is the man who longs for, works for, the Master's " W.D." : " Well done, good and faithful servant ", Matthew xxv. 23. It is a good thing to earn the applause of earth ; but how much more worth while to get the approval of heaven. That is " honour " indeed. One winter's morning, at a London railway terminus, a ticket-collector

was causing anger for demanding " All Seasons, please ", necessi-
tating the unbuttoning of coats and unwrapping of scarves. A
passenger passing his barrier remarked, " You're not very popular
this morning ". To which the official, pointing to the offices of
the General Manager of the Line, smilingly replied, " I don't
mind, Sir, so long as I'm popular up there ". Ah, it's good, if
maybe, to be popular with our fellows ; but what really matters
is to be " counted worthy " by GOD.

We note that (ii) *The test of their worth*—is twofold. In the
matter of Administration, do they " rule well " ? Have they
that strength of personality that can command respect and
obedience ; do they possess that business-like capacity that
ensures good order and real success ? One can imagine that in
those days of the early church, when everything was in the
beginning state, it required that men of considerable practical
gift should be in charge of affairs. Recall how necessary it became
to appoint " honest " men, in Acts vi. 3, to look after " this
business " of the widows' dole. All sorts of practical problems
would be constantly arising, which could only be ruled well by
men with a sound head for business. In the matter of Edification,
do they " labour in the word and doctrine " ? That, after all, is
the elder's chief function, and the measure of his attainment in
this sphere will be decisive in the judgment of his worthiness
or otherwise. Alas, some make very little effort of their preaching—they come to their pulpit ill-prepared ; the giving of their
message bears little evidence of the giving of themselves, it takes
little out of them ; but the elders here under review are " they
who labour " at it, for whom the sermon entails real toil. It is,
indeed, hard work—but it is none the less joyous work, this
proclamation of the " word " and promulgation of the " doctrine ". Laying the foundations and building up the super-
structure : these are the major responsibilities of those who seek
to edify the churches. By these, as well as by the arts of administration, is the leader to be assessed.

Next is discussed, (iii) *The reward of their worth*—" worthy of
double honour ", verse 17 ; " worthy of his reward ", verse 18.
There is material recompense ; and that is doubtless what is
referred to here—Gurney says, " honourable support, a sufficient
honorarium, paid by the congregation to its presiding presbyter " ;
and " double ", does not mean twice as much as was given to those
mentioned in the previous verse, it simply means " ample ".
This interpretation seems justified by the two quotations that
follow. The one from Deuteronomy xxv. 4, " Thou shalt not

muzzle the ox that treadeth [while he treadeth] out the corn "
—the animal is labouring for the food of man ; he shall himself
be fed, as he goes along. Do you think that is the point of the
" twelve baskets " of pieces of the barley loaves, in John vi. 13 ;
the Twelve had been busy about catering for the wants of others,
and now they shall be fed themselves—twelve baskets, one for
each of the Twelve ? Anyhow, the rule remains, that, as the
second quotation, from Luke x. 7, has it, " The labourer is worthy
of his hire " [or reward]. Yes, there is to be material remuneration
for the minister. I write as a pastor whose beloved church is
careful to see to this ; but there are congregations who are not
very mindful of this duty, and whose ministers have to drag out
a harassed existence accordingly, and cannot be expected to put
in their best work. If any church members or councillors
happen to read this whose consciences plead " Guilty " to this
indictment, will you see what can be done, and act quickly ? It
is not unseemly for me to write like this because, as I have said,
I happen to be one of the fortunate ones. I mentioned it just
now as a duty, but surely it should be something deeper, something sweeter, than this. Material reward ; but what of the
spiritual recompense ! How utterly and eternally rewarding a
pastor's life can be. Let this Paul himself testify to Timothy
and to the rest of us, after a long, and adventurous, and faithful
life of work and warfare—" Henceforth there is laid up for me a
crown of righteousness, which the Lord, the righteous Judge,
shall give me at that day, and not to me only, but to all them
that [so] love His appearing " that they shall wait and watch,
and work towards it, II Timothy iv. 8. Oh, all ye " elders " of
the churches, listen while I celebrate with you the gladness, both
here and hereafter, of our Master's service—the joy of working
not only for Him, but with Him, I Corinthians iii. 9 ; the joy of
knowing that our work will prove to have been not in vain,
Psalm cxxvi. 6 ; I Corinthians xv. 58 ; the joy of serving Him
with no unworthy element intervening, Psalm xxxii. 2 ; the joy
of leading a soul to CHRIST, Luke xv. 7, 10, a joy shared with
the very angels above ; the joy of the prize for fidelity, if we can
win it, Philippians iii. 14 , the joy of increasing light, right on to
the end of the road, Proverbs iv. 18. John Bunyan wrote of
" Grace Abounding " : what a companion volume he could have
given us on " Joy Abounding ". We " elders " may know these
joys and fruits, if we live and serve faithfully, as part of the
spiritual rewards of our labour. And now we must turn our
attention to a sad part of our passage—

THE REBUKE OF UNWORTHY LEADERS

Which is the theme of verses 19–21. Here are three things for our serious consideration. (i) *The possibility envisaged*—" them that sin ". But these are " elders " ! Yes, I know ; but, you see, the old root of sin remains in the best and to the end. You have only to turn to Galatians v. 17, or even to one day in your own heart's experience, to become aware of that fact ; and that being the case, it is not outside dark possibility that even the best may sink to even the worst. You remember the searching comment of the old great preacher, John Bradford, to a friend, as he saw a manacled prisoner being led away, " There goes John Bradford but for the grace of GOD ". There never comes a time when a man can afford to cease being watchful, or to bypass the " boundless stores of grace " available for his supply of strength. But, concerning this unworthy elder's sin, Timothy is to be on his guard against believing the matter too readily. The Old Law was careful to lay it down, in Deuteronomy xix. 15, that two or three witnesses were required to establish the truth of any such matter ; and so Paul says " receive not an accusation but before two or three witnesses ". Do you remember our Lord's same direction on the subject of a brother's trespass, in Matthew xviii. 16 ; and how, in Matthew xxvi. 59–60, His enemies tried so hard to get two witnesses to agree on some one point on which His supposed guilt could be established, and only at long last found two prepared falsely to testify together to something that He never said. This, then, was a safeguard in the disciplinary measures to be instituted against a guilty presbyter.

We come next to (ii) *The publicity enjoined*—" them that sin rebuke before all, that others also may fear ". The present tense, " them that sin " implies that the case is one of habitual falling. One sad sin may, perhaps, be dealt with, and hushed up ; but where a man continually yields to it, he has forfeited the right to a kindly secrecy; indeed, while he thinks that no one will know, it will encourage him in his wrongful habit. Moreover, he must now be used as a warning to others who might be tempted to think lightly of sin, and likely to fall into it. This publicity may be a very painful proceeding, but it will prove salutary in the end, if its effect is to pull others up sharp. What a striking instance of such publicity we have in the incident in which Achan's transgression was dragged out into the light, and he himself, with his family, punished in the eyes of all, Joshua vii. 16 ff. And how startling was the open treatment of Ananias and

Sapphira, upon which " great fear came upon all the church ", Acts v. 2. A worthy leader is to be an example to the flock ; an unworthy a warning to all.

Be sure to note, further (iii) *The partiality eschewed*—" observe these things without preferring one before another, doing nothing by partiality ". Such cases are to be judged as in the sight of GOD and of CHRIST, and of His holy angels—who, if they rejoice at the conversion of sinners, must weep at the confusion of saints ; and, in consequence, there must be nothing but exact rectitude in awarding praise or blame. This trial of Father, Son, and angels is found also in Luke ix. 26. The words translated " preferring " and " partiality " are interesting, and both imply prejudice : the first, is prejudice against the accused ; the other, is prejudice in favour of the accused. No, no ; away with them both, and let the judgment be entirely unbiased—facing all the facts, making all allowances, coming to free conclusions, awarding just penalties, whoever or whatever the accused may be. Ugly rumours will sometimes, quite unwarrantably, gather around a well-known name or person—an " elder " would be especially vulnerable to this kind of dastardly attack ; because of his leading spiritual position, Satan will sometimes seek to weave a web of suspicion around him. Let those who have to investigate be on their guard, lest grave injustice be done. Sometimes the rumours are only too well founded—then, again, without fear or favour, must justice be done ; and whose ever name be tarnished, GOD's Name be honoured. So, up against the background of the Rewards and Rebukes that we have been discussing, we come to look into this third important consideration—

THE RESPONSIBILITY OF CHOOSING LEADERS

The apostle deals with this vital problem in verses 22-5. We may take it for granted that, as the presiding presbyter of the wide area—diocese we should call it to-day—Timothy will have the onus of making many appointments to the headship of this or that church within his district ; and he would be both glad and grateful for the guidance offered him. It is a difficult passage ; but we must see what we can get out of it—not putting our own ideas into it, but trying to get GOD's thoughts out of it. Paul has been giving warning against prejudice and partiality, now he is up against precipitancy. " *Lay hands suddenly on no man* ". Ellicott thinks that this laying-on of hands refers to the restoration of penitents ; but, though in later times that ceremony was used in the readmission of backsliders, yet we never find it used in that connection in the New Testament, and, adds Gurney, " the context suggests that Chrysostom and the older commentators are right in regarding it as referring to ordination " of these elders. By the way, the " suddenly " might better be rendered as " hastily ". Suppose this caution were ignored, and without due enquiry and testing the elder turned out to be unsatisfactory, and positively sinful ? Then, in a very real sense, Timothy would be a "*partaker of* [*his*] *sins* "—by his unbecoming hurry in appointing the man to that church, he is to that degree and in a certain measure linked with the offender in responsibility for the wrong-doing that ensues. Now, says the apostle, " *Keep thyself pure* ", or free, from that unfortunate situation. I suggest that that is the meaning of the sentence in this context, rather than the more specific moral significance that we have, perhaps, generally accorded it. Sexual cleanness is enjoined elsewhere in the New Testament—personally, I think not here.

Then comes that curious advice to Timothy about his refraining from total abstinence—curious, that is, in its occurrence here. What has it to do with the argument ? Scholars have been at pains to try to make sense of its presence at this point. " *Drink no longer water, but use a little wine for thy stomach's sake and thine often infirmities* "—he is recommended not to be a water-drinker, almost a technical term, as we should say, an abstainer ; he was no longer to be a drinker of water only ; he was to begin to try wine medicinally. Note the strange word " use ", not drink, or take, but almost as if he were to limit it to a dose ; note also, only a " little ", not a lot. The Bible has many a warning about strong drink ; but Paul's suggestion here seems to be only a dietetic prescription for a weak digestion. But I have branched off from the subject of this verse's being found just here. Well, as I have said, many ideas have been put forward ; but, in my simple way, I wonder whether there is any need to link it up with the context at all. We too often forget that these Epistles are not ordered discourses, every part in its proper sequence, but letters, written, as with us, in a more loosely knit fashion. I offer you the suggestion that the last word of the previous verse has reminded him that Timothy's physical constitution is not one of pure strength and quality, his blood was not pure, and so, lest he should forget, while it is in his mind, he puts in this bit before resuming his thread in the verse following—just a parenthetical remark by the way.

The closing verses of the chapter are now before us. They are so difficult as almost to be cryptic, as they stand ; but perhaps a kind of paraphrase will bring out the meaning behind the words, if not of the actual words themselves. Perhaps the main drift of the verses is to demonstrate that in exercising the strategic duty of choosing men for the key posts in the churches, appearances, good or bad, are apt to be misleading. Let me then close our consideration of this important chapter of the Epistle by quoting to you a summary of these verses which I find in Dummelow's One Volume Commentary. It says, " Some candidates for ordination have characters so evidently bad that their unfitness is plain before probation ; in others it comes out later. And the same may be said of worthy candidates, some are plainly fit at first sight, others will be found fit on looking below the surface ". I believe that interpretation is justifiable. I am interested to discover that the late Canon Liddon, in his Analysis, takes very much the same line, stressing that Paul is urging upon Timothy the twin dangers of a falsely favourable estimate and a falsely unfavourable estimate of men, and the urgent importance of avoiding them both. How essential it is that leaders of the church shall be rightly and wisely chosen ; and that those whose task it is to make selection shall seek the great gift of spiritual discernment. Does it, I wonder, come within the content of that word " wisdom " in James i. 5. If so, there is glad hope for this seeker, since the endowment he needs is promised to believing prayer.

XI

MONEY MATTERS

I TIMOTHY vi. 3–10; 17–19

3 If any man teach otherwise, and consent not to wholesome words, *even* the words of our Lord Jesus Christ, and to the doctrine which is according to godliness ;

4 He is proud, knowing nothing, but doting about questions and strifes of words, whereof cometh envy, strife, railings, evil surmisings,

5 Perverse disputings of men of corrupt minds, and destitute of the truth, supposing that gain is godliness : from such withdraw thyself.

6 But godliness with contentment is great gain.

7 For we brought nothing into *this* world, *and it is* certain we can carry nothing out.

8 And having food and raiment let us be therewith content.

9 But they that will be rich fall into temptation and a snare, and *into* many foolish and hurtful lusts, which drown men in destruction and perdition.

10 For the love of money is the root of all evil : which while some coveted after, they have erred from the faith, and pierced themselves through with many sorrows.

17 Charge them that are rich in this world, that they be not high-minded, nor trust in uncertain riches, but in the living God, who giveth us richly all things to enjoy ;

18 That they do good, that they be rich in good works, ready to distribute, willing to communicate ;

19 Laying up in store for themselves a good foundation against the time to come, that they may lay hold on eternal life.

THE apostle has already had something to say concerning financial affairs, warning bishops against covetousness, iii. 3, and deacons about being greedy of filthy lucre, iii. 8 ; but now, in these two passages, he deals with the matter at greater length, and with more detailed particularity. There is quite a lot about money in the Bible, which only goes to show how true to life the Book is, for money, for many, holds pride of place in thought, in conversation, in ambition, in possession. So let us see what, through these verses Paul, as the agent of the HOLY SPIRIT, has to teach us on the subject. And first—

THE MONEY-GRUBBER'S PORTRAIT

There he is clearly depicted in verses 3–6. " Supposing that gain is godliness ", says our Authorised Version, of verse 5, as if, in their eyes, financial success is a veritable religion to which all their energies are completely dedicated " in full and glad surrender ", if we may so desecrate the old familiar words. Or if many of the scholars are right in inverting the words, " supposing that godliness is gain "—supposing that piety is a means of gain, or, as Moffatt renders it, " They imagine that religion is a paying concern ". Of course, in a sense that is true, " godliness with contentment *is* great gain ", verse 6, but not in the way these money-grubbers mean it. Profit is their ruling passion, and if a seeming religiousness contribute to that end, then " the devil a monk will be "—as if a grocer, a doctor, or even an undertaker should decide that attendance at church would prove to be good business. Such things have happened : though it must not for a moment be supposed that every church-going business or professional man is there for mundane or monetary advantage. Far be it, for many, many such men are true, practising Christians who seek in the congregation of GOD's people not wealth but worship. But those persons whom Paul mentions, and whom Timothy will meet, are wholly insincere—it is, with any luck, the lucre they are after.

With this at the core of his being, what kind of an individual is he likely to be ? (i) *The sort of person that will attach little importance to Scriptural teaching*—" consent not to wholesome words, even the words of our Lord JESUS CHRIST, and to the doctrine which is according to godliness ", verse 3. The true doctrine of godliness is so vastly different from his own flippant view of it ; and for this deeper concern he has no use at all ; if it do not increase his bank balance he will not, as he would think it, waste his time over it. The words of the mart and the exchange are the words that guide and goad him, while the wholesome words of our Lord carry no weight in his metallic soul. It was to just such a man as this that GOD said, " Thou fool ", Luke xii. 20, for this fellow, piling up his fortune, had no thought for his soul, and left GOD out of his reckoning—and any man is a fool who does that. Psalm xiv. 1 assures us that it is a fool that " hath said in his heart, there is no GOD ". To have no GOD in our heart is to have no sense in our head. When the twelve spies went in to spy out the land, a great cleavage developed between them : ten said, " We can't ", because they left GOD out, two said, " We can " because they put GOD in. For the former, the tragic sequence was no GOD, no land : they all ten died in the wilderness. Verily, it is a foolish thing to say, or to think, " There is no GOD "—or to act as if there weren't. It is the height of folly to ignore His wholesome words or His great teaching ; but these metallurgic men have no room, no use, for Him.

Another characteristic of this type is, that He is (ii) *The sort of person that will set little value on moral character*—" he is proud ", verse 5, but he has little reason to be, judging from the strictures that Paul passes upon him. What a list it is—" knowing nothing ", he thinks he does, but in reality he is sadly ignorant of things that matter most, of eternal things, of heavenly things, of spiritual things, of GOD's things ; " doting about questions ", giving his affection to questionable, debatable things ; " strifes of words ", with their bad progeny of envy, strife, and the like ; " evil surmisings ", wickedness of secret thoughts ; " perverse dis- putings ", continual friction ; " corrupt minds ", dwelling on base and unholy thoughts ; " destitute of the truth ", not a grain of the truth of GOD is in him, he breathes the very air of falsehood, " from such withdraw thyself ", he is so infected as to be in- fectious. You observe that there is no trace of any decency about him—no kindly thoughts, no gracious words, no helpful deeds. Come to think of it : don't you sometimes see something of all this on the very face of the inveterate gambler, a hard and coarse look, the glint of gold in his eye—or had we better say the passion of paper ?

A further feature about him is that he is (iii) *The sort of person that will give little thought to good influence*—" from such withdraw thyself ", verse 5, the writer felt bound to advise ; have no personal touch with him; he is a contagious person. Yet, the man will care nothing about what effect he is having on others. Tell him to pull up for the sake of others, and he will in all probability laugh or sneer in your face. What recks he of others ? All he thinks of is himself : his mathematical arithmetic may be by very reason of his employ, considerable: he thinks in thousands ; but his moral arithmetic has got no further on than Number One. His influence in society may be thoroughly bad ; and if you talked to him of a life making for good, he just couldn't compre- hend it, and certainly would not apprehend it.

Not a very attractive portrait, you will agree. But when Paul counsels that they shall withdraw themselves from such an one, does he mean that all contact shall cease, and that no attempt shall be made to lure him into better ways ? Well, there is that

intensely solemn utterance in Genesis vi. 3, when, as ushering in
the terrible Flood, GOD says, " My Spirit shall not always strive
with man "—the foreknowledgeable Lord knows when it will be
useless to attempt any further suasion, a point beyond which
there remains no hope. In a certain swift river in America, there
is a spot where a spur of land juts out, creating a narrower
channel—always rapid, the waters there pile and quicken themselves up into a positive cataract, and woe betide any boat or
person caught in the cruel current at that place. The spur of
land was called " Redemption Point " ; and any craft advanced,
perhaps in ignorance or perchance out of control, beyond that
spot was known to be helpless and hopeless, because, as was
said, it was " Past Redemption Point ". Yes, spiritually there is
such a condition when the soul is past redemption, for the
SPIRIT has ceased His striving. It is not for us to judge that any
man has reached that point ; but, alas, alas, there is the appalling
fact—when GOD gives him up ! Do you recall that devastating
decision of GOD's, in Hosea iv. 17, " Ephraim is joined to idols,
let him alone " ? It seems that that was for a time, for in xi. 8,
He says, " How shall I give thee up, Ephraim ? " But the dark
withdrawal of GOD we mentioned earlier is a thing for ever.
Remember the words of the apostle of love, in I John v. 16,
" There is a sin unto death : I do not say that he shall pray for *it* ".
Yet, such cases will likely be proportionately rare ; and the
warnings are probably recorded that man may be taught that he
mustn't play with sin, mustn't trifle with GOD. I suggest, then,
that Paul would have Timothy not cut all connection even with
the apparently hopeless case—we are not to be the companions
of such (" withdraw thyself "), but we are still to have a concern
for his soul, still to pray for him, still to take any chance he may
allow us to say a word, still to live before him a real, happy,
consistent Christian life, still working on, and hoping on, to the
end. It is time now that we turned to learn, from verses 7–10—

THE MONEY-GETTER'S PERIL

There is always the danger of (i) *A leaning to extravagance*,
verses 7–8—We arrived here " in this world " with no luggage of
material possessions ; when we take our journey hence, we shall
depart similarly unencumbered. All we shall take with us are the
spiritual things—our memories, Luke xvi. 25 ; our characters,
Revelation xxii. 11 : but material properties—no ! Why, then,
all this craze for riches : we cannot take them with us. Surely

the simpler outlook is the saner, " and having food and raiment, let us be therewith content." Life's essentials are very few— the two just mentioned, and but one or two more : what we put on, our raiment; what we put in, our food ; what we put up, a house to dwell in ; and what we put by, for our loved ones. A rich man, his money gotten, is always tempted to a degree of comfort which may lapse into luxury. Would that be right for a Christian ? Note that I ask, not answer, the question. Plain, simple content-ment is a beautiful quality. In the course of his Happy Letter, Paul says, " I have learned, in whatsoever state I am, therewith to be content ", Philippians iv. 11. It is one of the rich man's dangers that he lacks contentment—having got one thing, he wants another ; as the old proverb puts it, " Much wants More ". After all, he can afford it, so why shouldn't he have it ? Perhaps we shall be able to settle that point later on in this Study. As we said earlier, it is not wrong to have riches, of course not ; but only bear in mind that there is a danger of bloated and pampered extravagance.

Then there is (ii) *A temptation to shadiness*, verse 9—not, now, well-off, but " they that *will* be rich ". Who make up their mind to it ; who set all their gifts and energies towards it ; who are deter-mined to get money—honestly, if they can, but get money. There lies the temptation, the snare, the foolish and hurtful lust —to go to any lengths in order to become rich. What satis-faction do these " rich-at-any-price " men get out of their affluence ? Are they not snared from one shady transaction to another—losing their high integrity, and self-respect. Is it worth it ? This is here for caution, not accusation ; for it must not be supposed that this is the usual history of the wealthy—this is but to remind them that the temptation is there, to which some succumb, but over which many succeed.

Nor, in this connection, must we overlook (iii) *A danger of un-belief*, verse 10—It is often said, but not by Paul, that " money is the root of all evil ". That would be blatantly untrue, for, as a matter of fact and of human experience, money has been the root of much joy, much healing, much good, much kindness. Moreover, there is no definite article in the Greek, it is better to render " a root ", for there are other roots, besides money, from which evil grows. In addition, the " all " really signifies " all kinds of evil ". Chief point of all is, of course, that it is not " money ", but " *the love* of money " that is this evil root from which springs such evil fruit—most evil of all being that it some-times leads a man to give up his Christian faith. I myself know of such : men who, in their humbler days, were keen on GOD'S things, but who, as they got on in the world, and got up on the ladder of fortune, began to err from their old and simple faith in GOD, and eventually lost it all together. Many comforts have come to them by reason of their long purse ; but " many sorrows " will come to them in the day when they realise how foolish they have been. Luke xix. 25 is sufficient commentary on that point. Losing faith : what a sad tragedy, which would not have happened to these people but for " the love of money ". And what about that other peril, from the opposite point of view— the difficulty of gaining faith ? Think of that young man in the Gospel who was so eager for GOD'S best, but, rich as he was, couldn't pay the price—to " follow " CHRIST involved for him, though not necessarily for others, the surrender of his possessions : he just couldn't face the cost, and so he " went away grieved, for he had great possessions ", Mark x. 22. JESUS " loved " this young man—loved him too much to make discipleship easy for him. Perhaps he afterwards came back and believed, as some have guessed ; but, in any case, the comment of the Master, spoken sadly I feel sure, was, " How hardly shall they that have riches enter into the Kingdom of GOD ". It isn't impossible —many rich men have become sincere Christians ; but it is hard for them to do so, harder than for ordinary people. I must not pursue that theme further here ; for we must get on to another, and much brighter, aspect of this money business—

THE MONEY-GIVER'S PLEASURE

" Ye ought . . . to remember the words of the Lord JESUS, how He said, It is more blessed to give than to receive ", said Paul, in Acts xx. 35, to these very Ephesian elders over whom Timothy was to be appointed Chief. Writing now to that very man, as he takes up Office, about the joys of the Giving life, in verses 17–19 of our chapter, he opens the subject.

First there is to be recognised (i) *A decided sense of the Giver*, verse 17—Timothy will have a very rich section in his area, and will be called upon to meet, and to help spiritually, a number of well-to-do men. This would be especially difficult for a man so young as their Bishop. He has great responsibilities towards them, as towards others. They are to be urged to humble-mindedness, and not to rely on their money to secure for them position and comfort, for riches are always undependable—here to-day and, by some turn of fortune in business or investment, gone to-morrow.

Rather let their trust be in the living GOD—Himself the great Giver, because He is the great Lover. " GOD so loved . . . that He gave ", John iii. 16. It is in the very nature of love to give, and GOD is the great Exemplar of it. Legend has it that a certain country, in search of a king, sent two ambassadors to choose between two infant twins. They found the little fellows asleep, and they noted that one lay with his little fists tightly clenched, while the other had his hands wide open. It was the latter that was chosen ; and so great was his generosity that he became known in his country's annals as " the King with the Open Hand ". We have a GOD with an open hand for " He that spared not His own Son, but delivered Him up for us all, how shall He not with Him also freely give us all things ", Romans viii. 32 ; and as verse 17 of our passage says, " GOD . . . giveth us richly all things to enjoy ". Let these rich men, then, link up with the Great Giver, that they in their measure may have the joy of being great givers ; for let them ever bear in mind that, though they may talk as if it is wholly their own doing, really " it is He that giveth thee power to get wealth", Deuteronomy viii. 18. The world is made up of Getters and Givers—and all the lasting satisfactions are with the latter, especially if it is done in fellow-ship with our always Giving GOD.

So we go on to consider (ii) *A definite stewardship of the Gift*, verse 18—It is a grand thing to have money, if your chief idea is to "do good " with it, and not just occasionally, but continually, being " *rich* in good works "—that so your munificence become beneficence. So far as Christians are concerned, " This is a faithful saying, and these things I will that thou affirm constantly, that they which have believed in GOD might be careful to maintain good works ", so writes Paul, in Titus iii. 8. To do this is one of the greatest pleasures that belong to the giving-rich, as distinct from the getting-rich. They are " ready to distribute "—that is, to impart to the poor. Writing to members of Timothy's congregation, Paul says that each is to work hard " that he may have to give to him that needeth ", Ephesians iv. 28. " To give " is, in the Greek, the same as " to distribute ". What a joy is this, to be able to help some poor soul along the road : yes, not merely a duty, but a joy, for " the Lord loveth a cheerful giver ", II Corinthians ix. 7, or, as the word is, a " hilarious " giver—as if he found the very greatest happiness in doing it. And, moreover, they are " willing to communicate "—that is, to share in partak-ing. We might, perhaps, be permitted to draw the distinction between the two words by suggesting, by way of illustration, that " to distribute " is to send the poor man out something to eat, while " to communicate " is to invite the poor man in to share your meal with you. The rich man here visualised is " ready " to do the one, and even " willing " to do the other.

One more addition to his pleasure (iii) *A delightful sequel to the Giving*, verse 19—Giving away is here represented as a " laying up " in store, a laying down of a foundation. A time may come when he will be glad of some help himself, and to have amassed for himself in other hearts a great store of thankfulness on account of what he was able to do for them will stand him in good stead now that he is in want of sympathy, or assistance of any kind. One is reminded of that story that the Master told about the unjust steward, in Luke xvi. 1–9, whose " lord " commended him, verse 8—not " the LORD " : *His* comment comes in the verse following, " *I* say . . ." Mark what He did say : it is most interesting. Let me paraphrase it, by way of clearing up some of its difficulties. " Make to yourselves friends by the use of your money [which proved even the means of leading them to heaven] that, when you come to die, they may be there to welcome your arrival at the eternal resting-place." Ah yes, money laid out for the material help of the poor, and for the spiritual advancement of the kingdom, is treasure laid up in heaven, in accordance with CHRIST's own guidance in Matthew vi. 20. One thinks of Robert Browning's quaint little poem of The Twins, " Date and Dabitur " : Give ; and It shall be given you. The first being the elder of the twins !

So we come to the last part of this delightful sequel for the genuine givers—" that they may lay hold on eternal life ". We must let that word " eternal " go, for the Greek phrase is the same as we found in chapter v. 3, " widows indeed ", and we must, therefore, translate here, " life indeed "—lay hold on the life that is life indeed ! As my friend, Lindsay Glegg, would say, " Life with a capital L ". Possess to the full all the joys, powers, blessings, whether Here or Hereafter, of that Life which is theirs whose life is laid out for Him, and for others.

XII

A GODLY MAN'S SLOGANS

I TIMOTHY vi. 11–12

11 But thou, O man of God, flee these things; and follow after righteousness, godliness, faith, love, patience, meekness.

12 Fight the good fight of faith, lay hold on eternal life, whereunto thou art also called, and hast professed a good profession before many witnesses.

MANY a man has taken a sort of motto which has served him as a guide or inspiration through life—sometimes it is a family motto. Here are three words of the kind offered by Paul for Timothy's use, words which might well form the motto of the family of GOD.

You will notice the description by which our youthful bishop is here addressed—" Thou man of GOD " : not, it would seem, an official designation, but a spiritual characterisation. It is more likely to have been official in the Old Testament. Remember how it is applied to Elijah after his resuscitation of the widow's son, " Now by this I know that thou art a man of GOD ", I Kings xvii. 24. Elisha also is called by that noble name, " Behold now I perceive that this is an holy man of GOD that passeth by us continually ", II Kings iv. 9—this was said of him before he raised the child back to life. It was not any remarkable miracle that called forth the appellation in his case, but the holiness of his character, the godliness of his behaviour—a fine tribute, coming, as it did, from his landlady. If this was a Title, here was a man who lived up to it, which is not always the case. We call some men " Reverend "—when perhaps they are not at all reverent, or themselves worthy of reverence ; we call some women, " Lady "—when possibly they are " no lady ", with nothing ladylike about them ; we address some men, " Justice "—when perchance there is no trace of justice about their personal, and private, lives ; we may know a man as " King "—when, after all, he is no king, unless that, in the sense of Romans v. 17, he may be said to " reign in life ". Alas, it often happens that we fail to live up to our names. Take, for instance, the familiar phrase in Romans i. 7 (also in I Corinthians i. 2), " called *to be* saints "—where the " to be " is in italics, showing that it is not in the Greek, but is put in by the translators to give what they think is the meaning. But, are they right ? " Called saints ", would make perfect sense, and would be perfectly accurate, for that is what GOD does call believers, it is one of His names for them—you and I are called saints. Yes, but are the translators wrong ? Being called saints, we are called *to be* saints—to be what we are, to live up to our name. A prince living as a commoner, a rich man living as a pauper, a military officer living as a down-at-heels deserter—these would be eccentrics, you say ; a Christian living on a low level, no better than a worldling— this, too, is woefully eccentric. Those who are called saints are called to be saints ; a " man of GOD " should be living up to his title—as one who Believes on Him, Belongs to Him, and Behaves like Him. According to those terms, we can all earn the honourable title, whether the " aged " Paul, or the " youth " Timothy, or you, or me. We may be sure Timothy did, both before and after his appointment to take the helm of the See of Ephesus. And for his own personal life—both in private and in public— Paul gives him these guiding rules, the three slogans.

THE FIRST IS NEGATIVE—" FLEE ! "

Discretion is often the better part of valour ; and, not infrequently, the Christian's safety and wisdom is to run. " Flee these things ", says our passage, that is, this covetousness and its results, which have just been spoken of in the previous verses 9–10. We may, I think, legitimately enlarge the counsel, and urge that we shall turn our backs, and run away from anything that is calculated to spoil the Christian experience, to hinder the Christian progress, or to lower the Christian standard, anything that will cause the unwary believer to be content with anything less than the best. Surely the man of GOD will desire to be the best for GOD : that will answer many of his questions about doubtful things. " Flee "—yes, but whither shall we fly ? Let us go to Proverbs xviii. 10 for our sign-post, " The Name of the Lord is a strong tower : the righteous runneth into it, and is safe ". A provision akin to that of the six cities of refuge for the unintentional manslayer, in Numbers xxxv. 11. When any temptation comes, the secret of overcoming is not to stand and fight it : even a psychologist will tell you the danger of looking at it, having it on your mind, while purposing to fight it, which will gravely increase the likelihood of your succumbing to it.

No, the secret is to run away. Use the Name : at the moment of attack, turn to the Name—no need to pray, GOD knows what you mean when, either aloud, or within, you simply breathe the Name—it will indeed act as a " strong tower " of escape. But there are two conditions. (*a*) This is only for " the righteous ", or, as the New Testament would say, the believer. It is only the Christians who possess the key of the Tower ; and (*b*) There must be no dallying, the tempted one will be overtaken, and overcome, if he, as it were, strolls leisurely in the direction of his safety, that is, if he delays and trifles ; he will never reach the Tower unless, at the first thought, he immediately " runneth " —then, but then only, he " is safe ". " Oh safe and blessed shelter ", as the hymn says, and that in more senses than one. But, enough of our negative slogan—

THE NEXT IS POSITIVE—" FOLLOW ! "

In the Bible, the Christian life is never contemplated as a merely negative thing : it is, in all respects, a fundamentally positive thing. And so Paul lays it down here in his advice to his young pupil and comrade : he gives him six things that he should take pains to pursue—we may, perhaps, not unhelpfully, think of them as a sixfold relationship.

" *Righteousness* "—relation to our fellows. I think that always in the New Testament, when this word is coupled with the one following here, it bears this particular significance. What, then, of our relationship to the members of our family, and household—even Christian people are not always " right " in this, " right " with one another ; in a Christian home, alas, it sometimes happens that the members get across one another with constant friction, and consequent unhappiness. What of our relationship with our neighbours—is that " right " ? Do they find us kind, and ready to help whenever need arises ? Do we set before them a good example of consistent Christian behaviour ? And, by the way, do we pray for them ? The relationship will not be completely " right " if we fail in that. What of our relationship with those whose shops we patronise—is that " right " ? Are we domineering and demanding ; or are we courteous and considerate ? A lady in my congregation had this testimony from a shopkeeper, who told me one day, " She's a real Christian, she is ". What of our relationship with our fellow church members—is that " right " ? Or are we caught up in one of those cliques that do such harm in a congregation, forever criticising the parson and all his works, and backbiting many ? What of our relationship with those we work with—is that " right " ? Are we living up to our religious profession, or have they cause to say, " These Christians are a lot of hypocrites ; we know, we have one in our office, or workshop " ? Yes, Timothy, as church leader, must be careful to act righteously in all his human relationships ; and so must we.

" *Godliness* "—relation to GOD. Is His Word our constant study ; His Will our earnest endeavour ; His Work our happy employment ; His Worth our daily theme ? Is it our chief ambition that we may please Him ? I suppose that " godliness " means " god-likeness " : are there increasing evidences of a growing likeness, such as is contemplated, for example, in II Corinthians iii. 18, " We all, with open face, beholding, as in a glass, the glory of the LORD, are changed into the same image, from glory to glory, even as by the Lord the SPIRIT ". If our relationship to Him is " right ", that sort of transformation will be taking place in our character.

" *Faith* "—relation to duty. For faith here, as so often, represents faithfulness, fidelity. Can GOD, can others, depend on us ? My mind, in this connection, so often goes to I Kings xvii. 9, where GOD says to Elijah, " Behold, I have commanded a widow woman there to sustain thee ". This good lady had every excuse for pleading that she could not do what GOD asked of her—she was poor, with but " an handful of meal " in the cupboard ; yet she was told to feed this prophet in this time of famine. In the circumstances, how could she ? Ah, but, you see, GOD was part of the circumstances, so she could ! GOD knew He could rely on her. Can He trust us ? Our duty towards GOD : our duty towards our neighbour—are they faithfully fulfilled ? Do we keep our word, carry out our undertakings, fulfil our promises, discharge our obligations? Is there complete fidelity about us ?

" *Love* "—relation to all. Romans xiii. 8 says, " Owe no man anything, but to love one another ", as if to teach us that we ought —owe it—to have that overmastering feeling towards mankind at large. The Romans passage goes on to underline what our Lord Himself had stressed earlier, in Matthew xxii. 36–40, that, where love is, commandments are, we might say, automatically obeyed—if we love our neighbour, of course we shall not kill him, steal from him, tell lies about him. Law, and love. "Thou shalt . . . thou shalt not . . ." Yes, but how ? " Thou shalt love ". Love for the unknown, love for the unlovely, love for the unprofitable, love for the unfriendly—a Samaritan for a Jew. Those are the four facets of the priceless diamond of love, in Luke x. 30 ff. What a quality for the Timothys of the church to follow after. And the secret is in Romans v. 5.

" *Patience* "—relation to circumstances. The conditions of life can be very trying : as difficult, perhaps, for the present-day church as for the church of the first days, though, doubtless, in a different way. The slowness of advance, the opposition of unbelief, the weakness of members, the humdrum of life, the rarity of zeal, the perverseness of men, the subtlety of temptation —all these, and other problems, contribute to the difficulty of life for the Christian, in varying kinds and degrees, from age to age. Patience is the quality of holding on whate'er betide. In its New Testament use it means endurance—even of torture, and martyrdom. Timothy himself is reputed to have been, in the end, clubbed to death for his faith. It is little wonder that the word was sent to the believers of that age, " Ye have need of patience ", Hebrews x. 36. In our easier, but perhaps subtler days, let us seek to follow after this grace of persistency, of which we have already spoken in an earlier Study.

" *Meekness* "—relation to self. Some people seem to imagine that meekness is weakness. We can only suggest that they try it for a week. That will soon cure them of the delusion. Meekness is, in reality, the response to that challenge of the Lord JESUS, " If any man will come after Me, let him deny himself and take up his cross daily, and follow Me ", Luke ix. 23 : " deny himself ", say " No " to his self, cross himself out. It is as Paul has it in Galatians ii. 20, " Not I but CHRIST ". It is the obliteration of self ; the subservience of self to others, and especially to Him. Self can be one of our greatest problems—self-righteousness, self-confidence, self-will, self-seeking, self-importance, even self-pity. Meekness is the opposite of all that, the absence of all that. It is difficult enough for us ordinary people ; but it must be harder still for those who occupy high positions, like Timothy, about to take the helm of this ship " Ephesus " of the Royal Church Navy. He will do the best, anyone will do the best, if there is in the life what my friend, Canon Thorpe, describes as " the minimum of self, and the maximum of GOD ". Yes, it is so often the case that the Christian's main trouble is not so much sin, as self. The old grammar that we learnt at school said, First Person, I ; Second Person, Thou ; Third Person, He. The new grammar that we are set to learn, when we enter the School of CHRIST, is—First Person, He ; Second Person, Thou (others) ; Third Person, I.

That is meekness ! Put another way, there is a threefold secret of real joy—JESUS first, OTHERS next, YOURSELF last. Again, that is meekness. Oh, to be meek as our Saviour was—utterly selfless. Here, then, are the six points embraced by this positive slogan of the godly man.

THE LAST IS ACTIVE—" FIGHT ! "

From one point of view, that is, the personal aspect, we are not to fight, but to flee ; yet from the other point of view, it is a fight—a real conflict, in the army of the Lord, with the forces of the evil one. No one can doubt the fact who has read his New Testament with any care, for over and over again the simile of soldiering occurs. Our foes are portrayed, in Ephesians vi. 12, " we wrestle not against flesh and blood, but against principalities, against powers, against the rulers of the darkness of this world, against spiritual wickedness in [heavenly] places ". What a crowd to have to combat. Ah, but our complete accoutrement is ready—all we have to do is to put it on : the girdle of truth -of reality ; the assurance that we really are His soldiers. The breastplate of righteousness covered back, as well as front, with His righteousness. The sandals of peace—no grit to hinder our marching. The shield of faith—not the little one, but the big one, which was large enough for a man completely to hide behind. The helmet of salvation—to guard against intellectual onslaughts. The sword of the SPIRIT—the great offensive weapon, which the Christian soldier must learn how to wield. Daily sword-drill is called for. The greaves of prayer—the last bit of the armour, covering the legs and the knees. Regular knee-drill, as the Salvation Army calls it, is also required to fit the warrior for the war. Most important of all is our G.O.C., described in Hebrews ii. 10 as " the Captain of their salvation ". Assuredly, it is a fight ; and thank GOD, we are on the winning side, since we follow Him who " went forth conquering and to conquer ", Revelation vi. 2.

Well now, let us concentrate our attention on our verse 12, and see what it has to tell us respecting the conflict ; and first (i) *The Object of the fight*—" Fight the good fight of faith ". It should be " *the* faith " : it is a war for the advancement of the Faith ; for the extension of the Kingdom ; for the planting of the Flag of JESUS CHRIST in lands, and in lives, where Satan's standard now proudly flies ; for the capturing of prisoners for Him, whose bond-service is perfect freedom ; for the onward march of His glory throughout the world. Here is a cause worth striving for ; here is a cause worth suffering for. " Thou therefore endure hardness, as a good soldier of JESUS CHRIST ", says Paul, in his last letter, written to this same man, II Timothy ii. 3. Be prepared for any Cost to yourself, so long as the Cause may thereby be advanced, and so long as the Captain shall be pleased in it all. Our valour for His victory—and " thanks be to GOD, which giveth *us* the victory through our Lord JESUS CHRIST ", I Corinthians xv. 57.

So much, then, for our Object : now note (ii) *The Subject of the fight*—the one who is to wage it. We all come under that category, of course ; but the passage is speaking still of this Timothy, a Junior Officer in the Forces engaged in this World War. Two things are said about him—(*a*) " Whereunto thou art also called ", he had received his call-up papers. The Aorist tense of the verb tells us that it happened at a specific time—it was at his Recruiting Office in Lystra, at the moment of his conversion to CHRIST, when he became not only His servant, but also His soldier, unto his life's end. (*b*) " And hast professed a good profession before many witnesses "—not " a ", but " the ". It is, says Dr. Vincent, " important to preserve the force of the article, a point in which the Authorised Version is often at fault ". The good profession was doubtless his public baptism, the open confession of his allegiance to CHRIST. This—to pursue our military metaphor—was, as it were, the donning of His uniform, token of his having " joined up ", and of his now proudly taking his place in the ranks—unashamed and unafraid to be a member of such an army.

Which brings us, lastly, to (iii) *The Secret of the fight*—" Lay hold on eternal life ". Here the word " eternal " is to be retained, being in the Greek, unlike the phrase in verse 19, that we considered in one previous Study. It is the same " life ", but differently described. It is a life which, beginning now for the believer, goes on through eternity. Even here—

> " Before we upward pass to heaven
> We taste our immortality."

It was the entering on that life which was his enlistment in the Force ; now it is the laying hold on it which is his enlargement of strength for the fight. It is sometimes said of a very ill man that he has only a slight hold on life—he is alive, but only just. So it is with some Christians—delicate, invalid, ill : they have life, yes, but only a faint and feeble thing, so different from the Master's conception when He said, in John x. 10, " I am come that they might have life, and that they might have it more abundantly ". Strength sufficient for our soldiering comes, not only from just having the life, but from laying hold on it, getting such a grip on it as to secure our drawing into ourselves of all the virility, vitality, and victory that it can supply. It is in this sense that the apostle of love says, " This is the victory that overcometh . . . even our faith ", I John v. 4. My friend Montague Goodman has summed it up in the concluding lines of his thrilling hymn, set to Hudson Pope's exhilarating music—

> " The fight of faith our fight shall be,
> Till faith shall end, in sight, Lord ;
> As men of God we'll live for Thee,
> And *Flee* and *Follow* and *Fight*, Lord."

XIII

THINGS WORTH DWELLING ON

I TIMOTHY vi. 13–16; 20–21

13 I give thee charge in the sight of God, who quickeneth all things, and *before* Christ Jesus, who before Pontius Pilate witnessed a good confession ;

14 That thou keep *this* commandment without spot, unrebukeable, until the appearing of our Lord Jesus Christ :

15 Which in his times he shall shew, *who is* the blessed and only Potentate, the King of kings, and Lord of lords ;

16 Who only hath immortality, dwelling in the light which no man can approach unto ; whom no man hath seen, nor can see : to whom *be* honour and power everlasting. Amen.

20 O Timothy, keep that which is committed to thy trust, avoiding profane *and* vain babblings, and oppositions of science falsely so called :

21 Which some professing have erred concerning the faith. Grace *be* with thee. Amen.

WE have come to our last Study in this heart-to-heart missive sent by way of preparation, edification, and inspiration as Youth Takes the Helm. It has contained so much that must have proved of immense assistance to this young man who was called to the Oversight. And now three things remain to be said, three things that, if he forgot all else, it will be to his profit ever to keep in mind. The first we may call—

THE GOOD CONFESSION

In verse 13. We might, alternatively, call it " The Gospel Sovereign of Life ". You see, it was " CHRIST JESUS who . . . witnessed a good confession ". And when we observe the nature of it, we shall at once realise the wisdom of recalling it continually. Go back, then, to the records, and, in John xviii. 37, you read, " Pilate therefore said unto Him, Art Thou a King then ? JESUS answered, Thou sayest that I am a King. To this end was I born, and for this cause came I into the world, that I should bear witness unto the truth "—the truth of His Kingship obviously. Right at the start of His human life it was said that He was born . . . king ", Matthew ii. 2. At an early moment of His ministry, an excited crowd wanted to " make Him a King ", John vi. 15. Towards the end they witnessed that almost rehearsal of the Advent Royal Procession, and, quoting from the old prophecy of Zechariah ix. 9, they cried, " Behold, thy King cometh unto thee ", Matthew xxi. 5. At the close of that week came the mock-coronation in the soldiers' common-room, when they aped the usual homage with their studied insolence, " Hail, King of the Jews ", Matthew xxvii. 29. Then came the final scene, when, to the great annoyance of the Jewish leaders, Pilate had it nailed over Him on the Cross, " This is JESUS, the King of the Jews ", Matthew xxvii. 37. He has left this earth with His reign rejected, " We will not have this Man to reign over us ", Luke xix. 14 ; but He is to return " having received the Kingdom ", verse 15, at the Father's hand, and all the judgments, first, and then all the joys, of His oft-predicted Millennial Reign will begin. While we await this blissful con-summation, it is ours to seek to win for Him a throne in the individual lives of men and women and, above all, if that has never yet been done, to offer Him the throne of our own lives. After that we are, by lip and life, to make proclamation of His accession to that throne. A great difference between Christians lies in this—that in some He is only over the threshold, in others He is on the throne. Which is it with us ? Years ago the Student Volunteer Missionary Movement held a great Conference in Liverpool, when representatives from almost every University in the world were to be present. When the time arrived, however, something prevented the delegates from the Christian University of Japan from coming, but they promised to cable a message. In course of time it was received and read to the Conference with electric effect : it consisted of three words only—" Make JESUS King ! " I remember that a young Cambridge graduate, J. Russell Darbyshire—who recently died, as Archbishop of Capetown—was so thrilled by the message that he wrote, words and music, a chorus which had great vogue at that time, forty years ago. It ran—

> " ' Make JESUS King '—through Him we will live,
>   Our souls and our bodies to Him we will give,
>   His praises we'll sing, and others we'll bring,
>   Till the whole of creation shall ' Make JESUS King ' "

Here is, indeed, something worth dwelling on, His good confession of His Kingship before Pontius Pilate. He that was " born

Saviour ", Luke ii. 11—let us turn from sin and trust Him as such ; was also " born King ", Matthew ii. 2—let us crown Him with our love and devotion.

By the way, it may be mentioned in passing that we have an interesting instance here of the historical basis of our Christian religion, in the reference to CHRIST's appearance before Pontius Pilate. II Peter i. 16 says, " We have not followed cunningly devised fables when we made known unto you the power and coming of our Lord ". Other religions may be thus fancifully originated, but Christianity stands firm-footed on a rock of proven facts. The Incarnation is a mystery, so is the Crucifixion, so is the Resurrection, so is the Ascension, so is Pentecost—all Mystery, yes ; but all History. Well now, here is another thing worth dwelling on—

THE GREAT COMMANDMENT

In verses 14-16. We might describe it, otherwise, as " The Gospel Way of Life ". I think we may say that it is the way of love. Let me try to put that to you, for your consideration. Have you noticed how often in the New Testament that word " commandment " is used in an indefinite way—it is not explained, it is assumed that the readers in each case will understand which commandment it is that is referred to. Even in our verse 14, " Keep [the] commandment "—which one ? The context doesn't help us to an answer. Look at I Timothy i. 5, " Now the end of the commandment . . ."—which one ? The context throws no light on the matter. Look at II Peter ii. 21, " to turn from the holy commandment "—which one ? And iii. 2, " the commandment of us "—which one ? In neither case does Peter's context explain. Look at I John ii. 7, " I write no new commandment unto you, but an old commandment, which ye had from the beginning . . . Again a new commandment I write unto you . . ."—which one ? The immediate context has no solution, though the thing is unravelled later in the Epistle. I suggest that, among those first believers, there was one particular commandment, " the " one, which they would all recognise as what was meant. Now, go back to that passage we have already considered, Matthew xxii. 35-40— " Master, which is *the* great commandment ? . . . This is *the* first and great commandment, and the second is like unto it "— which one ? The context does help us here—" Thou shalt love . . . thou shalt love . . ." That I think answers our enquiry, and establishes the nature of the commandment here in our passage—a life of love. Note (a) How we are to keep it—" without spot, unrebukeable ". So often other people, and indeed our own conscience, accuse us of a lack of love in our thinking, our speaking, our acting, our refraining. Oh, that we might be so filled with the HOLY SPIRIT that we may be completely and conspicuously possessed with that love which is His fruit, Galatians v. 22. Note (b) How long we are to keep it—" until the appearing of our Lord JESUS CHRIST ". Beyond that there will be no need to exhort to love, because then love, being one of the three things that " abide ", I Corinthians xiii. 13, will be forever the very air we breathe. Till that blessed time, let the people of GOD " keep this commandment ".

How moving is the description given to Paul to utter of the GOD who is love, and from whom all love proceeds. The words seem almost to tumble over one another in their effort to express the inexpressible. And you will notice how that it is linked up with the thought of the Second Advent of CHRIST, which has just been referred to. " Which . . . He shall shew "—not the Son, but the Father, as at the end of verse 16. The Father shall display to the wondering eyes of men the glorious appearing of His Son coming for His own, and coming for His throne. " In His times "—GOD works for men to a time-table ; and there have been certain red-letter days marked on the Divine Calendar from the beginning—Christmas, " when the fulness of the time was come ", Galatians iv. 4 ; the HOLY SPIRIT, " when the day of Pentecost was fully come ", Acts ii. 1 ; Judgment, " He hath appointed a day in which He will judge the world ", Acts xvii. 31, and so with the Second Advent, " That day and hour knoweth . . . My Father ", Matthew xxiv. 36. It is not for us to know the date, any day now may be the day, and we are meant to be ever on the alert, lest that day take us unawares. A solicitor friend of mine, to keep him on the qui vive, has on his office desk a little framed card, bearing the words, Perhaps to-day ! But there it is, in the Calendar, and it will all happen " in His times ". Happy the people who, in that day, shall be found living in love. " Blessed and only Potentate, the King of kings, and Lord of lords " —the latter titles are given also to the Lord JESUS, in Revelation xvii. 14, and xix. 16, showing His co-equal Deity with the Father. Compared with the little potentates of earth, the " only " Potentate ; and the Potentate whose potency lies chiefly in blessing. " Who only hath immortality "—it is in Him, by essence ; in us, by gift. Mark that reference in II Timothy i. 10

to the Lord JESUS, " Who . . . hath brought life and immortality to light [out into the light] through the gospel ".
Again we contemplate our GOD " *Dwelling in the light which no
man can approach unto* "—we can't approach to the sun, but we
can walk in the sunshine ; even so we may, and must, " walk
in the light, as He is in the light ", I John i. 7, and thus have
blessed fellowship with Him, the Sun of Righteousness ", Malachi
iv. 2. " *Whom no man hath seen, nor can see* "—GOD had said
to Moses, " Thou canst not see My face : for there shall no man
see Me and live ", Exodus xxxiii. 20. Moses had asked to be
shown His " glory ", instead GOD made His " goodness " to pass
by. We turn to John xiv. 9, where our Lord, in answer to
Philip's request " Shew us the Father ", says. " He that hath
seen Me hath seen the Father "—no immediate vision of GOD is
possible to human sight, but the vision is mediated to us through
the Son. We may, anyhow, know what the Father is like by
looking at the Son. Turn now to I John iv. 12, where, as it
seems to me, we have something very suggestive, " No man hath
seen GOD at any time. If we love one another, GOD dwelleth in
us . . ." What, do you think, is the connection between those
two sentences ? Is it not that though no man can see Him
directly, they can see something of Him indirectly in Christians
who have His love in their hearts? If my exegesis is right, what
a mighty privilege is ours, what a solemn responsibility, that in
our degree we may, as our Lord in His perfect way, show the
world something of what GOD is like.

The other day I came across these lines by a Scotch poet,
Thomas Crawford—

> " Who thinks to look at the Sun,
>   But strikes himself blind !
> His zeal doth his wisdom outrun,
>   And leave it behind !
> Let him look at the earth, with its wonderful store
> Of light and of colour, of beauty galore ;
> Its blossom and fruit, its pure joys evermore—
>   And what's hid in the Sun he will find !
>
> Who thinks to look upon God,
>   For nought his strength spends ;
> To search for Him, after such mode,
>   In vanity ends !
> Let him look where, resplendent, in lives all around,
> Truth, purity, love, deeds unselfish abound—
> Which never in Nature's own garden were found—
>   And what God is, he soon apprehends."

How true when the " lives " are clean enough, and close enough to reflect Him.

" *To whom be honour and power everlasting. Amen* "—such are His never ending prerogatives ; but, even now, we believers recognise that all the power we need, for all we ought to think, and say, and do, and be, comes from Him, and therefore, that for whatever be accomplished for us, in us, or through us, all the honour should be given to Him—just as Paul himself, in speaking of his marvellous conversion, says, " They glorified GOD in me ", Galatians i. 24—not me, but GOD ! You get the same thing in Matthew's recording of the close of what we call " The Lord's Prayer "—" For Thine is the kingdom, and the power, and the glory, forever ", Matthew vi. 13, to which is added there, and in our passage, our fervent " Amen "—It is so ! Let it be so ! Here, then, so beautifully and so bountifully described is the One who will " shew " us the " appearing ", and who meanwhile requires us to show the life of love. We are ready now to examine the third of these things worth dwelling on—

THE GREAT COMMISSION

In verses 20-1. We might entitle it " The Gospel Message of Life ". " O Timothy "—all the deep affection of his heart is in the syllables as he breathes them out, almost as a cry, to his amanuensis. His loving care for his pupil and protégé, his realisation of the dangers to which he will be exposed, his comprehension of the immense spiritual possibilities of his position, all these combine to fill this cry with utmost urgency. How he longs that his young Timothy shall have the best, do the best, be the best, for GOD. So now, as he dictates his last words for the moment, it is to lay upon him afresh the Great Commission, " Keep that which is committed to thy trust "—guard the deposit. A great deal has been written by way of attempting to decide what was the character of that trust committed to Timothy ; many suggestions have been offered. For my own part, I believe that the truth is in I Thessalonians ii. 4, " We were allowed of GOD to be put in trust with the Gospel ". First, put in touch with it— as the hand of faith grasped the Saviour, who is Himself that gospel. Next, put in tune with it—as, by the HOLY SPIRIT, our lives correspond to the life that the Gospel demands. Then, put in trust with it—as we are now held responsible for passing the good news on to others. What a commission for Timothy, and for Paul, and for all us lesser folk.

In connection with the propagation of this gospel message of life, the apostle has three recommendations to make, all which are to be taken to heart by all elders, all preachers and teachers, all believers. The first is (i) *Resist the temptation of those who try to steal*—" Keep . . . thy trust ". The figure is that of a banker guarding safely the moneys, the jewels, the securities committed by his customers to his care. With what vigilance and diligence he will see to their security, and outwit the evil intentions of any who will try to " break through and steal ", Matthew vi. 19. As the custodian of the faith for that Ephesian church, let their Overseer be at least as watchful as that banker, and see to it that none shall rob the church of any part of the truth, or the believer of any portion of its blessing. Many temptations may come to water down the message ; but these, from whatever quarter they arise, are to be strenuously resisted.

Another piece of advice Paul has to offer is (ii) *Avoid the discussion of those who want to argue*—" avoiding profane and vain babblings ". Judging from one's own experience, one would dare to say, " and a very sensible piece of advice, too ! " Argument about scriptural and spiritual things never got anyone anywhere. The facts of Christianity are matters of revelation, not of reason —the rôle of reason is to elucidate the truth, not to establish it. Besides, argument is largely a matter of clever and quick wits— you may be beaten in argument and yet be right. So often this form of discussion can only be characterised as " profane ", since it is flippant about serious things, and " vain ", since it is profitless for progress. No, don't argue ; stick to your message. Don't waste time arguing about the seed—sow it !

One further suggestion (iii) *Ignore the opposition of those who think they know*—" oppositions of science falsely so called ". The word " science " gives a somewhat misleading impression : it just means " knowledge " of any kind, and not that particular department to which the name " science " is usually applied. I do not propose to discuss here the relation between science and religion, except to remark that there appears to be taking place a gradual, and as yet a slow, " rapprochement " between the two. A wise conservatism does not exclude a patient and thorough investigation to establish the accurate text of Scripture, and the truth thereby conveyed, and we so-called " old-fashioned " believers have nothing to fear from such reverent search. But all this is beside the point of our passage, which deals only with the knowledge " falsely so called ". There is a flippancy, an arrogance, about some who speak and write about religion that fills us with wonder, especially in the case of otherwise reputable scholars. To hear some of them lecture on their own subject of philosophy, or science, is a sheer intellectual delight, most re- freshing and stimulating to the mind ; but when, as they do, they enter on the field of the Christian religion, they are at once out of their depth, as we said in our third Study—they think they know ; and they speak with such assurance that they lead many of the younger generation astray by their knowledge " falsely so called ". Many have " erred concerning the faith ", because they have supposed that such men, magnificently supreme in their own department of thought, are necessarily to be trusted as supreme in all fields. Let any who are bewildered by these clever " oppositions " learn the truth of that statement in I Corinthians ii. 14, which I quote again, " The natural man [that is, the man who is not a Christian] receiveth not the things of the SPIRIT of GOD, for they are foolishness unto him ; neither *can* he know them [though he thinks he does], because they are spiritually discerned "—not naturally, not intellectually, but spiritually. That's why it is that many an uneducated man has a wonderful understanding of spiritual truth—spiritual discern- ment ! Nothing that I have said is to be taken as an under- valuing of true science or knowledge—that would be foolish, and, indeed, the height of ignorance and impertinence. I speak only of the " falsely so-called " varieties.

Well, the time has come to say " Good-bye ", and Paul says it with the beautiful word " grace ". That was the first word the apostle said to him here, I Timothy i. 2, and now it is his last—" the sound of a great Amen ". It is as if the Epistle were a valuable book, with two exquisitely tooled covers—the front cover is " Grace ", and the back cover is " Grace ", the two binding the whole book together. And the intervening pages so largely take their colour from their cover. They speak of GOD's *Attitude* towards us—an attitude of grace ; they tell of GOD's *Assistance* of us—an assistance of grace ; they present to us pictures of GOD's *Attractiveness* in us—an attractiveness of grace. All these things the word means, as Ephesians ii. 5, 8 ; I Corinthians xv. 10 ; and Acts iv. 33 respectively declare. The grand old apostle, knowing all it implies, all it has meant in his own life, can think of no greater word to finish with, and the HOLY SPIRIT, who has inspired him all through, leads him to it.